MBLEX TEST PREP 2024-2025

Mastering Massage Therapy | Your Essential Guide to
Passing the MBLEX - Complete Study Strategies,
Practice Exams, and Post-Exam Steps

VERE SIMONDS

TABLE OF CONTENTS

INTRODUCTION

MBLEx serves as a standardized measure of competency, designed to evaluate your understanding and readiness to practice safely and effectively within the field of massage therapy. Passing this exam grants you not only licensure but also the confidence and credential to stand out in an industry where skill and trustworthiness are paramount.

The MBLEx represents more than just a hurdle to cross; it is a milestone signifying excellence and dedication. In an industry that emphasizes wellbeing, adhering to a recognized standard assures clients of your commitment to their health. This exam evaluates your knowledge in areas critical to successful practice — from anatomy and physiology to ethics in massage therapy. In doing so, it ensures that all licensed professionals share a comprehensive and deep-rooted foundation.

Our book is structured meticulously, mirroring the actual content outline of the MBLEx, guiding you through chapters on Anatomy, Pathology, Techniques, Ethics, Business Practices, Client Assessment and much more. Whether you're grappling with muscle contraction mechanisms or navigating client communication intricacies, this guide provides clarity.

Furthermore, each chapter intertwines detailed subject matter with strategic study advice tailored for serious candidates. We demystify complex concepts with clear explanations and reinforce learning with practice exams mirroring real test conditions. Our ultimate aim is not simply for you to pass the MBLEx but to emerge as a well-prepared professional poised to enrich lives through massage therapy.

As you turn each page of "MBLEx Exam Prep," know that it has been meticulously crafted to pave a clear path toward success on your examination and confidence in your professional capabilities thereafter. Let this introduction serve as your first step into a committed practice that enhances lives—one therapeutic touch at a time. Are you ready to turn your passion into a professional reality? Let's begin.

HOW TO USE THIS GUIDE

This guide is designed to streamline your study process, provide key insights into the format and content of the exam, and offer strategies to enhance your test-taking confidence. As you embark on this journey towards professional certification, it is crucial to understand how to navigate through the guide effectively.

1. **Familiarizing Yourself with the Content Layout:** Begin by reviewing the table of contents, where the chapters are organized to mirror the MBLEx test structure. Each chapter delves deeply into a specific topic that you will encounter on the exam. You'll find comprehensive coverage of subjects ranging from Anatomy and Physiology to Ethics and Business Practices.

Each chapter is structured to facilitate both learning and revision:

> ➢ Clear headings and subheadings allow you to locate topics quickly.
> ➢ In-depth explanations ensure a thorough understanding of complex concepts.
> ➢ Practical examples illustrate how theoretical knowledge applies in real-world massage therapy settings.

2. **Developing an Effective Study Plan:** As outlined in Chapter 2, constructing a personalized study plan is vital. Consider your current knowledge base, learning style, and available time before crafting your schedule. Build regular study sessions into your routine, set achievable goals, and use this guide as a roadmap for your preparation efforts.

3. **Engaging with Practice Exams:** Chapter 11 presents multiple practice exams that are formatted similarly to the actual MBLEx. These simulate exam conditions and familiarize you with question styles you'll encounter. Use them judiciously; first studying the corresponding content before testing yourself, then using your results to identify areas needing further review.

4. **Enhancing Test-Taking Skills:** Chapter 12 is devoted to test-taking strategies that can make a significant difference in your performance. Learn how to approach multiple-choice questions efficiently, manage your exam time effectively, and remain calm under pressure.

5. Continual Resources for Learning: In Chapter 13, we provide additional resources including recommended books, study guides, online materials, and practice tests beyond this guide—ensuring you have access to diverse tools suitable for all facets of learning.

6. Understanding Post-Exam Procedures: Lastly, Chapter 14 outlines steps following the actual exam—how you'll receive scores and what follows upon passing.

Remember: success on the MBLEx doesn't merely come from memorizing facts; it's about understanding concepts deeply enough to apply them in practical scenarios. This guide serves as a mentor on your path—use it wisely by actively engaging with its content rather than passively reading it. Take notes, highlight key points, discuss topics with peers or instructors, and most importantly—apply what you learn through hands-on practice whenever possible.

You now hold a comprehensive toolset in *"MBLEx Exam Prep."* Approach each chapter methodically; leverage practice questions to assess comprehension; sharpen test-taking abilities via strategic advice provided herein; and complement this guide with external resources when necessary. Stay committed, stay focused—and success will be within reach!

CHAPTER 1
UNDERSTANDING THE MBLEX

The Massage & Bodywork Licensing Examination (MBLEx) is a standardized test created by the Federation of State Massage Therapy Boards (FSMTB). It serves as an assessment tool to determine the qualifications of candidates seeking licensure to practice therapeutic massage and bodywork. The examination evaluates a candidate's knowledge, skills, and abilities that are considered fundamental for safe and effective entry-level massage therapy practice.

The MBLEx is designed to be relevant across the United States, providing a uniform standard for licensing authorities. It covers topics such as anatomy and physiology, kinesiology, pathology, client assessment, massage and bodywork modalities, ethics, and guidelines for professional practice. The exam is structured into sections, each focusing on specific domains essential for proficient practice in the field.

Candidates taking the MBLEx can expect a rigorously developed test that has undergone extensive review by experts in massage therapy education and regulation. The purpose of this comprehensive evaluation is to protect public safety by ensuring that only those who have adequately demonstrated their knowledge are licensed to provide therapeutic massage services.

Each question on the MBLEx is multiple-choice, with four possible answers from which to choose. This format allows test-takers to demonstrate their understanding of concepts by selecting the best answer given a particular scenario or statement. While this might seem straightforward, it requires a deep understanding of theoretical and practical application in massage therapy.

The MBLEx is administered at Pearson VUE testing centers located throughout the United States. Candidates can schedule their exam at a convenient time after receiving authorization from their state board or the FSMTB once they meet eligibility requirements. The results of the MBLEx are recognized in almost every state, making it widely accepted among regulatory boards.

WHY IS THE MBLEX IMPORTANT?

MBLEx acts as a gatekeeper, ensuring that only those who have met specific educational standards and possess a baseline level of competency can enter the field. This serves several critical functions within both the profession and its interaction with consumers:

1. It aids in maintaining a standard of professionalism within the industry. By requiring prospective therapists to pass this test before obtaining licensure, it reinforces that individuals claiming to be professionals have a certain knowledge base.
2. Because the MBLEx is used extensively across various states with different local laws and regulations, it helps harmonize standards across jurisdictions. This means that therapists have greater mobility to work in different regions without having to take numerous exams specific to each state.
3. Clients can rely on consistent care quality since therapists have been vetted through a standardized process before receiving their permits to practice. In an age where consumer protection is paramount, providing assurance through rigorous testing is essential.
4. Finally, by upholding high standards for licensure candidates via testing such as the MBLEx, professional confidence grows both within and outside the field of massage therapy. It helps ensure therapists are viewed with respect by healthcare colleagues from other disciplines while offering clients clarity regarding therapist qualifications.

The examination is not just an academic hurdle but rather an integral part of ensuring public safety and professional integrity within massage therapy. By thriving through an evolving compilation of questions that reflect current industry knowledge and best practices, candidates demonstrate their readiness to offer effective services within this dynamic healthcare modality.

CHAPTER 2
PREPARING FOR THE MBLEX

The first key step to taking your Massage & Bodywork Licensing Examination (MBLEx) is the registration and scheduling process. Becoming a licensed massage therapist is within reach; however, it requires careful attention to detail as you begin your preparations. Start by visiting the Federation of State Massage Therapy Boards (FSMTB) website, which provides comprehensive information about the registration procedure.

Your initial task is to create an account on the FSMTB website. This portal serves as your center for all things related to the MBLEx. Once you are logged in, you'll find clear guidance on how to submit your application, as well as a checklist of required documents such as education transcripts and identification. Remember that the requirements may differ from one state to another; hence, it's crucial that you understand these particularities.

Payment of fees is an integral component of the registration process. The FSMTB site outlines current fees as well as methods of payment. Ensure that you are prepared for this financial aspect in advance to avoid any last-minute hurdles that might delay your exam plans.

With your application submitted and fees paid, next comes scheduling your exam date. You have a 90-day window in which to take the test after receiving your Authorization to Test (ATT) letter.

Locations and time slots may vary based on test center availability, so immediate scheduling is advantageous to secure your preferred date and site.

Time management becomes vital at this stage; planning well ahead provides you the liberty to choose a date that aligns with your anticipated level of preparedness. Picking a test date can be strategic too — some candidates prefer scheduling later within their 90-day window to allow maximum study time while others select an early date to maintain momentum after completing their massage therapy program.

DEVELOPING AN EFFECTIVE STUDY PLAN

Transitioning from registration to actual exam preparation brings forth another challenge: crafting an effective study plan tailored for MBLEx success. An effective study plan must be realistic, comprehensive, and flexible.

Assess your individual needs based on strengths and weaknesses in various content areas covered by MBLEx such as anatomy & physiology, pathology, kinesiology, ethics & standards of practice among others. Reflect honestly on where you excel and which areas require extra effort; this will direct the distribution of study time appropriately. Creating a detailed schedule can significantly enhance your study efficiency. Identify days and times most conducive for uninterrupted learning —for many, this might mean carving out regular early morning hours before daily responsibilities unfold or late evenings when interruptions are at a minimum.

Compile quality study materials from reputable sources including textbooks recommended by FSMTB or other recognized authorities in massage therapy education. Utilize practice exams extensively; these not only familiarize you with types of questions encountered but also benchmark progress. Practice tests should be taken under conditions emulating actual exam environments: timed sessions without access to notes or textbooks.

Integrate different learning styles into your routine - visual aids like charts or diagrams for anatomy reviews can be complemented with auditory methods such as educational podcasts during commutes. Kinesthetic learners may benefit from hands-on practice or teaching concepts they're studying to peers.

Remember that breaks are just as important as study sessions — overloading yourself can lead to burnout and diminish effectiveness over time. Regular breaks allow for restorative mental downtime which enhances long-term retention rate. Regular self-assessment should steer your plan's evolution – recognize when adjustments must be made either because certain topics have become strengths or focus areas need more intensive review than initially expected.

Finally, maintaining a positive mindset throughout this journey cannot be overstated; positivity impacts motivation levels and overall mental well-being significantly influencing learning outcomes.

CHAPTER 3
MBLEX CONTENT OUTLINE

ANATOMY AND PHYSIOLOGY

Anatomy and Physiology form the cornerstone of any massage therapy practice. This expansive field deals with the structure of the human body and how its various systems operate both independently and collectively.

Beginning with cells, the basic unit of life, we explore their structures and functions. Understanding how tissues form from cells to create organs, each with specific roles, establishes a foundation for comprehending bodily functions. The study extends to organ systems, including muscular, skeletal, nervous, endocrine, cardiovascular, lymphatic, respiratory, digestive, urinary, and reproductive systems.

In preparation for the MBLEx, it's important to focus on how these systems interrelate. For instance, consider how the respiratory and cardiovascular systems collaborate to oxygenate blood or how the muscular and skeletal systems work together to facilitate movement. Comprehension of homeostasis—how the body maintains a state of internal balance—and the mechanisms of feedback loops that regulate this balance is vital.

Furthermore, a good grasp of terms related to directions (anterior, posterior), positions (supine, prone), movements (flexion, extension), and planes (sagittal, transverse) is necessary as they are frequently referenced in therapy discussions and client interactions.

KINESIOLOGY

Kinesiology deals with body movements and mechanics – an essential area for any practicing therapist. A substantial portion of your studies should be devoted to understanding how muscles function synergistically during movement and stabilization.

In this segment of your exam preparation, focus on skeletal muscle anatomy—comprehending muscle origins (where they start), insertions (where they end), actions (what movements they produce), innervations (the nerves that supply them), and palpations (feeling muscles through the skin). Additionally, it is critical to review joint types (synovial joints like ball-and-socket or hinge joints), joint structures such as ligaments and tendons, as well as range of motion concepts.

Knowing specific muscle groups and their corresponding actions enables you to tailor massage techniques effectively. Remember to understand proprioception—the awareness of body position—and kinesthetic sense which guides coordinated movements.

PATHOLOGY

Pathology in massage therapy covers diseases and disorders that can impact a client's health status—and by extension—the approach required during therapy sessions. For MBLEx exam success in this category, study general pathology concepts which outline how diseases develop along with understanding inflammation processes as a response mechanism by the body against injury or infection. Learn about different modes through which diseases are spread; contamination, invasion by pathogens like viruses or bacteria or inherited genetically through DNA anomalies.

Next delve into systemic pathology—a study which must go hand-in-hand with that of Anatomy and Physiology since many systemic conditions like circulatory or neurological disorders have direct implications on therapeutic practices.

Crucially for potential therapists; know contraindications—an appreciation for conditions under which massage would not be recommended—or situations requiring adaptation in technique to ensure client safety.

MASSAGE AND BODYWORK ASSESSMENT

Assessment involves the evaluation of a client's current condition to formulate an effective treatment plan. The MBLEx tests your understanding of assessment techniques, including data collection through client intake forms, health history, and interviewing. Further, it examines your knowledge of visual assessments such as posture analysis, gait assessment, and body mechanics.

For effective assessment, you also need to master palpation skills to identify tissue health, abnormalities, or contraindications for massage. This includes feeling for temperature changes, swelling, or pain response. Moreover, you'll be tested on range-of-motion evaluations to assess joint mobility and muscle strength or weakness.

The exam will question your ability to integrate information from assessments to make informed massage and bodywork choices. It expects you to identify indications and contraindications for specific massage techniques based on your findings. Being adept with assessment ensures you can adapt your approach to optimize client outcomes while providing safe and effective care.

ETHICS AND PROFESSIONALISM

Ethics are the moral principles guiding our behavior; in massage therapy, they ensure we act in our clients' best interests while fostering trust within professional relationships. MBLEx content related to ethics covers confidentiality standards, boundary issues including dual relationships and sexual misconduct, and how to handle ethical dilemmas.

Professionalism extends beyond ethics into the broader scope of behavior expected in professional settings. You'll need to demonstrate knowledge of key attributes like timeliness, dress code adherence consistent with safety and hygiene standards, effective communication with clients and colleagues, record keeping consistent with legal requirements, and continued professional development.

Understanding ethics extends also to managing business practices ethically—discussing fees transparently before services are rendered and avoiding false claims about treatments or benefits. The FSMTB includes questions that test candidates' abilities to recognize ethical issues and choose appropriate actions that uphold professional standards.

GUIDELINES FOR PROFESSIONAL PRACTICE

The final section encompasses laws governing practice—a critical aspect because regulations can vary significantly from state to state. You'll be expected to identify general scopes of practice along with state-specific rules where you intend to work.

Also included in this section are hygiene practices essential to prevent cross-contamination or spread infections in a clinical setting. Hygienic practices cover proper handwashing procedures before and after each session, sanitizing equipment between clients, using clean linens for each new client, properly disposing waste products like oils or lotions used during sessions.

Finally, guidelines call attention to proper documentation practices—detailing treatment plans provided to each client along with subjective findings or objectives set for future sessions. Accurate record-keeping is integral not only for legal compliance but also for tracking client progress over time.

CLIENT ASSESSMENT, REASSESSMENT, AND TREATMENT PLANNING

The initial step in any therapeutic relationship is an effective client assessment. This process involves gathering vital information through health history forms, client interviews, and physical assessments such as range of motion tests or palpation. Knowing how to interpret this data is indispensable for identifying treatment goals and contraindications.

Furthermore, reassessment serves as an integral component after initial treatments are provided. It allows therapists to evaluate the effectiveness of their strategies and revise treatment plans accordingly. A comprehensive treatment plan should include the primary objectives for therapeutic intervention, technique selection, session duration, frequency of visits, as well as measurable outcomes to monitor progress.

The primary aim here is to tailor each session to the client's unique needs by continually updating their profile based on ongoing assessments and feedback. This evolves a static treatment plan into a dynamic framework capable of adapting to changes in a client's condition.

BENEFITS AND PHYSIOLOGICAL EFFECTS OF TECHNIQUES

Understanding how different massage techniques impact the body physiologically offers insights into their benefits – an essential knowledge domain for any massage therapist. For instance, Swedish massage is famed for its relaxation effects and increased blood circulation while deep tissue massage targets chronic muscle tension.

Studies also show that massage can trigger endorphin release that assists with pain management, reduce stress hormone levels like cortisol, and promote parasympathetic nervous system activity which aids in body restoration.

Visualization techniques during a massage session may further amplify the healing process since it assists clients in connecting mentally with the physical work being done. Thus, examining these effects not only aids students in selecting appropriate techniques but also equips them with explanations that substantiate their therapeutic choices both during the exam and in clinical practice.

CONTRAINDICATIONS, AREAS OF CAUTION, SPECIAL POPULATIONS

One cannot overstate the importance of being well-versed with contraindications for massage therapy; that is knowing when it is not safe or beneficial to proceed with certain techniques or treatments due to potential harm they could cause. Common general contraindications include conditions like acute inflammation, severe osteoporosis, or contagious skin diseases. In contrast, local contraindications might restrict you from working on areas affected by recent injuries or surgeries.

Adeptness at identifying 'Areas of Caution' — points requiring special care or modified approaches such as avoiding deep pressure over varicose veins — is also mandatory for ensuring client safety and comfort. Moreover, special populations such as pregnant women or elderly clients necessitate adaptations in technique application and positioning during a session due to their distinctive needs. Familiarity with guidelines specific to these groups ensures that care remains individualized and efficacious.

OVERVIEW OF MODALITIES AND THEIR EFFECTS

In any therapeutic scenario, comprehending the modalities, or methods of therapy, available to a massage therapist is fundamental. Modalities in massage therapy are varied techniques and methods used to manipulate tissues for therapeutic purposes. They are designed around principles that target specific client needs and conditions.

Swedish Massage is considered the most common modality and involves five main strokes. These strokes include effleurage (gliding), petrissage (kneading), tapotement (rhythmic tapping), friction (cross-fiber), and vibration/shaking. This modality aims to promote relaxation, enhance blood circulation, relieve muscle tension, improve lymphatic drainage, and aid tissue repair.

Deep Tissue Massage works on deeper muscle layers to release persistent muscle tension. Techniques like slow strokes-directed pressure helps treat muscle pain arising from overuse or chronic conditions.

Sports Massage tailors techniques like stretching, compressions, and cross-fiber strokes coupled with an understanding of athlete training patterns. It's aimed at enhancing performance while preventing or treating injuries.

Shiatsu and Acupressure depend on concepts from traditional Chinese medicine that work along meridians identified as energy pathways. These modalities involve applying pinpoint pressure to facilitate energy flow called 'Qi,' treating various physical ailments.

Aromatherapy employs essential oils blending with massage lotions or oils having different therapeutic effects such as calming or energizing.

The modalities mentioned are just a few examples out of numerous options available in massage therapy practice. Each has effects tailored towards specific treatment goals whether targeting relaxation, injury recovery or alleviating chronic conditions.

CLIENT COMMUNICATION AND DRAPING

Crucial to any therapeutic relationship is proficient client communication and appropriate draping techniques ensuring comfortability as well as privacy. As a therapist, maintaining open channels for feedback regarding discomfort or personal preferences during sessions is imperative.

Initial consultations often require the therapist to explain the chosen modality—addressing how it operates—and ensure understanding and consent before proceeding. Successful draping involves covering areas not currently being massaged with a sheet or towel ensuring only one part of the body is exposed at a time hence maintaining modesty.

BOUNDARIES, LAWS, REGULATIONS, AND BUSINESS PRACTICES

Boundaries are set guidelines upholding professionalism within therapist-client relationships—preventing harm while fostering a safe environment for both parties involved through establishing clear lines between professional services and personal interactions.

Furthermore, adhering strictly to laws is non-negotiable in ensuring ethical operation while protecting all parties involved legally. This includes abiding by state regulations regarding licensing while also being aware of scope-of-practice limitations—all therapists must be up-to-date with these stipulations ensuring they only offer services their license permits.

Business practices touch upon managing logistics such as scheduling appointments—maintaining accurate client records—and executing savvy marketing strategies building one's clientele base sustainably within legal parameters provided by industry standards as well as local business laws.

ETHICS

Ethics in massage therapy encompass principles such as beneficence—promoting good; nonmaleficence—not causing harm; autonomy—respecting an individual's right to self-determination; justice—providing fair treatment; and fidelity—maintaining trust by truthfully outlining one's qualifications without misrepresentation.

It's imperative for therapists to understand ethical decision-making processes when confronted with dilemmas such as accepting gifts from clients or managing instances when a contraindication for massage is apparent.

A rigorous commitment to ethics also implies continued professional development through education and staying abreast of research in the field—an obligation not only for personal growth but also for ensuring competent practice.

By integrating these topics into your study routine, you will build a solid foundation not just for passing the MBLEx but also for a rewarding career in massage therapy. Successful navigation through these topics prepares you for a responsible role where you can offer therapeutic benefits within a safe, respectful environment—exemplifying what it means to be a well-rounded massage therapist ready to serve your community with skill, integrity, and compassion.

CHAPTER 4
ANATOMY AND PHYSIOLOGY

THE MUSCULAR SYSTEM

The human body is a marvel of biological engineering, and at the heart of our physical capabilities lies the muscular system. This intricate network of muscles is responsible for every movement we make, from the powerful beat of our hearts to the delicate blinking of our eyes. Muscles are classified into three types: skeletal, smooth, and cardiac. Skeletal muscles are voluntary muscles attached to bones and controlled consciously to facilitate movement. Smooth muscles form the walls of internal organs and blood vessels, and their involuntary contractions help regulate bodily functions. Cardiac muscle is found exclusively in the heart, where it propels blood throughout the body with rhythmic contractions.

Each skeletal muscle is composed of thousands of fibers, which are the basic units of contraction. These fibers are bundled together by connective tissue to form muscles. Within each fiber are myofibrils containing sarcomeres—the true workhorses of muscle contraction. Sarcomeres consist of overlapping thin (actin) and thick (myosin) filaments that engage in a molecular handshake known as a cross-bridge. It is this cross-bridge cycle that facilitates muscle contraction.

The partnership between muscles and nerves begins at neuromuscular junctions where motor neurons release neurotransmitters that bind to receptors on muscle cells. This binding triggers an electrical impulse that courses through the muscle fiber, instigating a contraction.

Muscle Contraction Mechanism

The process of muscle contraction can be intricate but understanding it is essential:

1. An action potential (electric signal) arrives at a motor neuron's axon terminal.
2. ACh is released into the synaptic cleft at the neuromuscular junction.
3. ACh binds to receptors on the sarcolemma (muscle cell membrane), causing a change in permeability.
4. This change allows sodium ions to enter the muscle fiber rapidly while potassium exits, creating an action potential in the muscle fiber.
5. The action potential travels down T-tubules deep into the sarcoplasm.
6. This triggers calcium release from the sarcoplasmic reticulum.
7. Calcium binds to troponin on actin filaments; tropomyosin shifts exposing binding sites for myosin.
8. Myosin heads attach to actin forming cross-bridges and pull actin filaments inward — this is when contraction occurs.
9. ATP provides energy for myosin heads to detach from actin and re-cock for another pull.
10. In absence of an action potential, calcium ions are reabsorbed and tropomyosin re-blocks actin's binding sites stopping contraction.

There are several types of muscle contractions you must understand for the MBLEx exam:

1. Isometric contractions occur when muscles exert force without changing length—think holding a yoga pose.
2. Isotonic contractions involve changing muscle length—as seen in lifting weights—classified further into concentric (muscle shortening) and eccentric (muscle lengthening under tension).

To sustain contractions muscles require energy primarily from ATP generated via three pathways:

1. Direct phosphorylation using creatine phosphate provides rapid but short-lived energy.
2. Anaerobic glycolysis breaks down glucose without oxygen creating ATP quickly but generates lactic acid.
3. Aerobic respiration requires oxygen breaking down glucose into more ATP than anaerobic methods but at a slower rate—ideal for endurance activities.

Aside from motion muscles also maintain posture providing protection around vital organs. Stabilizer muscles keep joints stationary during activity while synergist muscles support primary movers—the major muscles executing movements.

As a massage therapist preparing for MBLEx, you should be aware that common muscular system injuries include strains (overstretched or torn muscles) and sprains (ligament damage). Rhabdomyolysis is severe strain leading to breakdown of muscle fibers releasing myoglobin into bloodstream potentially causing kidney damage. These injuries may present with pain, swelling, reduced function/motion keeping massage therapists vigilant on contraindications.

THE SKELETAL SYSTEM

The human skeletal system is a remarkable and complex structure, essential to our mobility, protection of internal organs, and overall bodily function. Comprising 206 bones in the adult body, the skeletal system serves as the framework for the human body and plays a vital role in our everyday lives.

Bones are living tissues, constantly undergoing a process called remodeling, where old bone tissue is replaced by new. This process requires a balance between the actions of osteoblasts, cells that build bone, and osteoclasts, cells that break down bone. Proper functioning of this remodeling process is crucial for maintaining bone density and strength.

The skeletal system can be divided into two parts: the *axial skeleton* and the *appendicular skeleton*. The axial skeleton includes the skull, vertebral column, ribs, and sternum. It provides support and protection for the brain, spinal cord, and thoracic cavity organs. The appendicular skeleton encompasses the limbs and girdles. It allows humans to interact with and manipulate their environment with movements facilitated by joints that provide flexibility.

Joints are classified by their structure and function. Structurally there are three types of joints: fibrous, cartilaginous, and synovial. Fibrous joints have no joint cavity and are connected by fibrous connective tissue; these joints allow for minimal movement. Cartilaginous joints are slightly movable joints connected entirely by cartilage. Synovial joints are the most common joint type in the body; these have a joint cavity filled with synovial fluid that allows for free movement.

Synovial joints differ in types: hinge joints such as those found in the elbows and knees permit bending and straightening actions; ball-and-socket joints found in hips and shoulders allow for rotation; saddle joints as seen in thumbs permit grasping motions; pivot joints like those between cervical vertebrae enable turning of the head.

An understanding of how muscles attach to bones through tendons is essential when learning about the skeletal system's role in movement for massage therapy administered during MBLEX practices.

Bones not only support movement but also have critical roles in other bodily functions. Red blood cells are produced in the marrow of certain bones in a process called hematopoiesis, which is vital to delivering oxygen throughout the body.

Bone health can be influenced by various factors such as diet, exercise, hormonal status, age, genetic predisposition to certain conditions like osteoporosis – a disease where decreased bone density increases fracture risk. Nutrition plays an important role in maintaining bone health; adequate calcium intake is particularly essential for supporting strong bones.

Far from being inert structures of an anatomical framework, bones and their capacity to remodel underpin human growth from infancy through adulthood as well as repair following injury.

Pathological conditions affecting bones range from fractures – which need careful realignment and stabilization – to chronic diseases such as arthritis or osteoporosis.

Massage therapists preparing for MBLEX will need an intricate understanding of each bone's location and its potential points of attachment with other skeletal elements or muscles because this knowledge influences therapeutic strategies to alleviate discomfort or correct dysfunctions within the musculoskeletal system.

The upper extremity includes clavicles (collarbones), scapulae (shoulder blades), humeri (upper arm bones), radii (forearm's lateral aspect), ulnae (forearm's medial aspect), carpals (wrist bones), metacarpals (hand's palm bones), phalanges (finger bones).

Lower extremity comprises pelvic girdle (hip bones), femurs (thigh bones), patellae (kneecaps), tibiae (shinbones), fibulae (calf bones next to tibia), tarsals (ankle bones), metatarsals (foot's arch bones), phalanges (toe bones).

Recognizing these individual components' interrelationships gives valuable insight into their collective function within human motion.

THE NERVOUS SYSTEM

The human body is an immensely complex and intricate system, requiring a sophisticated network to coordinate its myriad functions. The nervous system is this vast command network, governing everything from our thought processes to involuntary responses like our heartbeat. To understand how the body operates, especially in the context of massage therapy and bodywork, understanding the basic anatomy and physiology of the nervous system is crucial.

The nervous system is broadly divided into two main parts: the central nervous system (CNS), which consists of the brain and spinal cord, and the peripheral nervous system (PNS), which encompasses a web of nerves that spread throughout the body. Each part plays a distinct role, with the CNS being the control center that processes information, and the PNS acting as a communication line that relay messages between the CNS and different parts of the body.

The nervous system relies on specialized cells, known as neurons, to transmit signals. Neurons are uniquely structured for this job; they consist of a cell body containing the nucleus, dendrites that receive signals from other neurons, and an axon that sends signals away. The space over which neurons communicate with each other is called a synapse. At these synapses, electrical impulses triggering neurotransmitters' release enable signals to be passed on to target cells. This process happens at incredible speeds, allowing for near-instant communication throughout the body.

To maintain homeostasis and smooth operations in various systems within our bodies, neurons work together in pathways or circuits. Sensory (afferent) neurons carry information from sensory receptors in various parts of our body to our CNS. The brain interprets these signals, and motor (efferent) neurons carry commands from the CNS to muscles and glands to instigate a response. This unilateral flow from sensory neurons through interneurons in the CNS to motor neurons forms what is known as a reflex arc - an essential component in immediate reactions to external stimuli.

A considerable portion of our PNS consists of two subsystems: somatic and autonomic nervous systems. The somatic nervous system controls voluntary movements like walking or dancing by sending signals from your CNS to skeletal muscle fibers; it's also involved with processing sensory information that requires conscious thought or awareness.

In contrast, the autonomic nervous system oversees involuntary actions inherent to survival - heart rate regulation, digestive processes, respiratory rate, pupillary response, etc. It operates independent of conscious control and is further divided into sympathetic (which prepares your body for 'fight or flight' emergency reactions) and parasympathetic divisions (which promote 'rest-and-digest' activities that occur when your body is at rest).

Neuroglia or glial cells are another key component; while they don't transmit impulses like neurons do, they provide structural support for neurons and maintain homeostasis within cerebrospinal fluid among other functions.

It's important for those preparing for MBLEX exams to appreciate how stressors can affect this intricate system. Stress induces activation of the sympathetic division leading potentially to overall health deterioration over time if not managed well. As massage therapists work closely with these systems via manipulation of muscles and connective tissue which influence nervous system activity indirectly by reducing stress levels or directly by virtue of neuromuscular techniques – manipulation can lead sensory receptors send calming signals up through PNS affecting overall balance favorably.

Understanding diseases or dysfunctions concerning neurological pathways – such as multiple sclerosis where myelin sheaths deteriorating slow down message transmissions in CNS can inform therapeutic approach choice.

Diseases like Parkinson's disease – resulting from dopamine-generating neuron death leading motor skills impacts – knowing this informs tailored approaches too.

Preparing for MBLEX entails having firm grip over neural anatomy physiology – ensuring effective compassionate care giving across varied client issues involving muscular skeletal pain migraines more all potentially rooted aberrant neural functioning.

THE CIRCULATORY SYSTEM

The circulatory system facilitates the transportation of blood, nutrients, gases, and wastes throughout the body, stands as a testament to the complexity and efficiency of human physiology. It encompasses the heart, blood vessels, and approximately five to six liters of blood that the heart moves through the circulatory system.

At the heart of the circulatory system is, quite literally, the heart. This muscular organ beats tirelessly—typically over 100,000 times per day—to pump blood throughout your body. It's divided into four chambers: two atria on top and two ventricles below. The right side of the heart receives deoxygenated blood and pumps it to the lungs for gas exchange, while the left side receives oxygen-rich blood from the lungs and pumps it to all other parts of your body. Valves between each atrium and ventricle ensure that blood flows in one direction, making each heartbeat a coordinated effort. Furthermore, conducting tissues like the sinoatrial node and atrioventricular node orchestrate contractions to maintain a steady rhythm.

Veins, arteries, and capillaries create an extensive living maze through which blood passes to deliver life-sustaining substances. Arteries carry oxygenated blood away from the heart to tissues and organs. Capillaries are fine networks where exchange occurs; oxygen and nutrients diffuse out while carbon dioxide and metabolic wastes are absorbed for removal. Finally, veins return deoxygenated blood back to your heart. It is crucial for therapists to recognize these pathways in order to anticipate how facilitative or relaxing their interventions might be.

Blood itself carries multiple critical components including red blood cells (RBCs) which transport oxygen using hemoglobin; white blood cells (WBCs) which are central to immunity; platelets implicated in clot formation; plasma which is a liquid containing numerous proteins like albumin; hormones; enzymes; nutrients like glucose; electrolytes; and waste materials.

Often not considered part of the circulatory system but undeniably vital is the lymphatic system. It manages fluid levels in your body, absorbs certain types of nutrients, and defends against invasive microorganisms alongside white blood cells found in lymph nodes.

Understanding circulation is not just academic—it has profound clinical implications particularly when considering conditions like hypertension (high blood pressure), varicose veins caused by valve failures within veins leading to swollen veins especially in legs, or atherosclerosis where plaques build up within arteries restrict flow leading potentially to heart attacks or strokes.

As massage therapists deeply familiarize themselves with circulation dynamics, they can positively influence various local circulation patterns through techniques promoting venous return or relaxation cycles influencing arterial flow. Knowledge about hot or cold treatments impacting vessel dilation or constriction can further enhance therapeutic outcomes.

Lifestyle choices can significantly impact circulatory health—choices about smoke-free living, maintaining appropriate weight ranges through regular exercise and diet management rich in whole grains, fruits, vegetables as well as lean meats or alternative protein sources play pivotal roles.

THE LYMPHATIC AND IMMUNE SYSTEMS

The lymphatic system is a complex network of vessels, ducts, nodes, and organs that facilitate the movement of lymph—a clear fluid rich in white blood cells. The primary structures within this system are the lymph capillaries, which merge to form larger lymph vessels that transport lymph throughout the body. Lymph nodes are small, bean-shaped structures scattered along the pathways of lymph vessels. These nodes house lymphocytes and macrophages that serve as filters, trapping bacteria, viruses, and other foreign particles.

Lymphatic organs include the spleen, thymus, tonsils, and Peyer's patches within the small intestine. The spleen filters blood and helps fight infections. The thymus is the maturation site for T-lymphocytes (T-cells), crucial for adaptive immunity. The tonsils protect against pathogens entering through the mouth or nose while Peyer's patches survey intestinal contents for potential threats.

Immune System: Innate and Adaptive

The immune system can be divided into innate (non-specific) immunity and adaptive (specific) immunity. Innate immunity provides immediate defense against infections through physical barriers such as skin, chemical deterrents in bodily fluids like saliva or stomach acid, and immune cells that react promptly to invaders. This includes phagocytic cells like macrophages that engulf pathogens.

Adaptive immunity involves a more targeted response where specific antibodies are produced to fight off particular pathogens. T-cells are responsible for cell-mediated immunity while B-cells handle humoral or antibody-mediated immunity—both critical for long-term protection after exposure to antigens.

Both branches work synergistically — without innate responses holding off initial infections, adaptive responses would not have time to develop sufficient defenses.

Interaction between the Lymphatic and Immune Systems

Lymph nodes serve as meeting grounds where immune cells encounter antigens collected by lymphatic vessels. B-cells can become activated here to produce antibodies or memory B-cells that respond more effectively upon subsequent exposures to the same antigen.

T-cells also activate in response to antigen presentation by special cells called antigen-presenting cells (APCs). Once activated, T-cells proliferate and carry out various functions including killing infected host cells and regulating other components of the immune response.

An understanding of the linkage between the lymphatic and immune systems is fundamental for massage therapists due to its impact on health conditions they may encounter. Manual lymph drainage can be a beneficial technique in cases where lymphedema—the accumulation of lymph due to obstruction or damage—is present. A strong immune response is vital during infections but can become problematic when misdirected as seen in autoimmune disorders or allergies.

Knowledge about allergens or contraindications for clients with compromised immune function ensures safety during treatment planning.

Inappropriate stimulation of these systems may exacerbate conditions like acute infections or inflammation. Recognizing signs of systemic infection such as fever or localized inflammation is paramount since these warrant referral to a medical professional rather than massage therapy.

CHAPTER 5
KINESIOLOGY

UNDERSTANDING JOINT MOVEMENT

Joints, or articulations, are points at which two or more bones meet. They are constructed to allow for varying degrees of movement and stability. Some joints afford a wide range of motion like those found in our shoulders and hips, while others offer firmness and support such as our knee joints. The joint structure includes components such as bones, cartilage, synovial membranes, ligaments, tendons, and bursae which work in concert to administer smooth and coordinated movements.

Bones serve as the rigid structures that form a joint. Cartilage is a type of connective tissue that covers the ends of each bone to facilitate ease in gliding against one another without friction. The synovial membrane is an enclosed sac that secretes synovial fluid for lubrication within some joints. Ligaments are tough bands of connective tissue that connect bones at a joint; hence they provide stability by preventing excessive movement. Tendons attach muscles to bones, enabling force transfer that produces movement at joints. Bursae are sac-like structures filled with synovial fluid cushioning between bones, tendons, and muscles around a joint.

Joint movements are categorized into different types: Gliding occurs when flat bone surfaces slide over one another as seen in some hand and foot movements. Angular movements increase or decrease the angle between two bones. Flexion reduces the angle whereas extension increases it; abduction moves a limb away from the body's midline while adduction does the contrary.

An illustrious example of angular movement is seen with circumduction - a conical movement pattern where one end of an appendage remains relatively stationary while the other end describes a 360-degree conical path - a combination of flexion, abduction, extension, and adduction performed sequentially as seen in shoulder circles.

Moreover, rotational movement facilitates a bone's pivoting around its own longitudinal axis as depicted by shaking your head 'no'. In addition to [these] fundamental movements, there exist specialized motions restricted to particular joints such as supination (turning palm upward) and pronation (turning palm downward) performed by radial and ulnar bones in forearm.

Functional categorization classifies joints based on their range of motions: Synarthrosis offers no movement intended for stability (e.g., skull sutures); Amphiarthrosis presents limited movement mainly for shock absorption or transitional areas (e.g., vertebral discs); Diarthrosis provides free-moving articulations known as synovial joints endowed with ligaments providing mobility and security (e.g., hip joint).

Movement in synovial joints is orchestrated through muscle contractions which can be isotonic – where muscle tension remains fairly constant while muscle length changes – resulting in either concentric contraction (muscle shortens) or eccentric contraction (muscle lengthens). Conversely, isometric contractions see no change in muscle length only tension increases such as holding a squat position.

Understanding how joint movement occurs can inform massage practices during MBLEX preparation both theoretically & practically. When treating clients within this purview effectively entails acknowledging each client's unique anatomical predispositions thus applying appropriate techniques targeting care within these parameters while avoiding damage or exacerbating existing conditions.

The study of kinesiology embodies not just anatomical understanding but also physics principles grasping how forces are applied during activities; biomechanics is vital such as leverage when standing from seated position leveraging lower body strength against gravity's pull understanding these dynamics assists therapists assisting clients optimizing their rehabilitating exercises or maximizing performance within safety confines.

MUSCLE FUNCTION AND ACTION

Muscles are the motors of the body that facilitate movement by contracting and exerting force on the skeletal system. There are over 600 muscles in the human body, which can be categorized into three types: skeletal (voluntary), smooth (involuntary), and cardiac (involuntary). For the MBLEX exam, the focus is predominantly on skeletal muscles and their functions. Skeletal muscles can perform four primary actions:

1. **Concentric contractions:** This occurs when a muscle shortens in length and develops tension. An easy way to visualize a concentric contraction is thinking about a bicep curl; as you lift the weight upwards, your bicep muscle shortens.

2. **Eccentric contractions:** Unlike concentric contractions, eccentric contractions occur when a muscle elongates while under tension. This is often experienced during the downward phase of lifting exercises – for example, lowering your arm back down after completing a bicec curl.

3. **Isometric contractions:** In this type of contraction, there is no change in muscle length but tension does increase. An illustration would be holding a weight steady in front of you without moving it up or down; even though there's no motion, your muscles are working hard to hold the position.

4. **Isokinetic contractions:** These happen when a muscle contracts and shortens at a constant speed. These types of contractions usually require specialized equipment to maintain the constant speed against variable resistance.

Understanding these functions allows one to grasp how muscles interact during different activities. For instance, when walking or running, muscles work in a synchronized manner through concentric and eccentric movements to provide propulsion; meanwhile, other muscles maintain balance through isometric contractions.

Another crucial concept to understand for the MBLEX exam is muscle origin and insertion points:

1. **Origin:** This is typically the proximal (closest to the center of the body) attachment site where the muscle begins.

2. **Insertion:** The distal (farthest from the center of the body) attachment site where the muscle ends.

Muscle fibers run between these two points. When they contract, they pull on bones at insertion points to generate movement at joints.

Awareness of these anatomical landmarks helps identify which muscles are involved in specific actions and what type of joint movements they produce:

1. **Flexion:** Decreasing an angle between two bones or bending.

2. **Extension:** Increasing an angle between two bones or straightening.

3. **Rotation:** Moving around an axis.
4. **Abduction:** Moving away from the midline or center line of the body.
5. **Adduction:** Moving toward the midline or center line of the body.

Each muscle has specific roles depending on its location in relation to joints they cross over:

1. **Agonist (or prime mover):** The main muscle responsible for producing a specific movement.
2. **Antagonist:** Muscles that oppose or resist against movements produced by agonists.
3. **Synergists:** These assist agonists in carrying out their actions and sometimes fine-tune movements to make them smoother.
4. **Stabilizers:** They support or stabilize one part of the body so desired movements can be performed in other parts.

For example, during elbow flexion (like when performing a biceps curl), biceps brachii acts as an agonist while triceps brachii will act as an antagonist preventing overflexion; meanwhile synergistic muscles such as brachialis assist in this motion without directly causing movement themselves.

This knowledge not only helps massage therapists identify which techniques are best suited for addressing clients' needs but it also underpins their ability to design effective treatment plans based on individual muscular functions and imbalances.

CHAPTER 6
PATHOLOGY

COMMON MUSCULOSKELETAL DISORDERS

These disorders affect a vast array of individuals, and knowledge about them is essential for proper diagnosis, management, and treatment. It is estimated that musculoskeletal conditions are among the leading contributors to global disability. Hence, recognizing the signs and symptoms, as well as understanding the underlying pathophysiology, is important for massage therapists in their practice. Moreover, this knowledge ensures therapists can provide safe and effective treatments and can help in guiding clients to appropriate medical care when necessary.

1. **Osteoarthritis:** Osteoarthritis is the degradation of joint cartilage and underlying bone, most common from middle age onward. It causes pain and stiffness, especially in the hip, knee, and thumb joints. The risk factors include aging, joint injury, obesity, and genetics. There is no cure for osteoarthritis, but management includes pain relievers such as acetaminophen or NSAIDs, physical therapy to strengthen muscles around joints, and sometimes joint replacement surgery.

2. **Rheumatoid Arthritis:** Rheumatoid arthritis is an autoimmune disorder that predominantly affects joints but can also have systemic effects. Symptoms include tender, warm, swollen joints and morning stiffness that may last for several hours. It's more

common in women than men and can result in bone erosion and joint deformity. Treatment options encompass immune-suppressing medications like DMARDs and biologics alongside corticosteroids and NSAIDs to reduce inflammation and pain.

3. **Fibromyalgia:** Fibromyalgia is a condition characterized by widespread musculoskeletal pain accompanied by fatigue, sleep problems, memory issues, and mood swings. While the cause isn't fully understood, it's believed to involve amplified painful sensations due to changes in how the brain processes pain signals. Treatment often includes both medication—such as pain relievers and antidepressants—and self-care strategies like stress reduction and exercise.

4. **Tendonitis:** Tendonitis is inflammation or irritation of a tendon – the thick fibrous cords that attach muscle to bone. Commonly affected tendons include those in the shoulder (rotator cuff tendonitis), elbow (tennis elbow), wrist (De Quervain's disease), knee (jumper's knee), or heel (Achilles tendonitis). Overuse or repetitive motion typically causes tendonitis. Treatment involves rest, ice application to reduce inflammation, compression with bandages to immobilize the tendon during healing; elevation to reduce swelling; NSAIDs for pain relief; physical therapy; and perhaps corticosteroid injections.

5. **Carpal Tunnel Syndrome:** Carpal Tunnel Syndrome is caused by pressure on the median nerve within the carpal tunnel of the wrist; it may result in numbness, tingling sensation in the fingers, weakness of the hand muscles responsible for thumb pinching movements. It can be brought on by repetitive hand movements or conditions that cause swelling like diabetes or rheumatoid arthritis. Initial treatment may involve wrist splinting especially at night, corticosteroid injections or anti-inflammatory medications; severe cases might demand surgical intervention.

6. **Lumbar Radiculopathy (Sciatica):** Lumbar radiculopathy more commonly referred to as sciatica when affecting sciatic nerve roots emanating from L4-S1 spine levels manifests as shooting pain from the lower back down through legs owing to nerve compression often button-like spinal disc herniation or stenosis—narrowing of spinal canal. Clinical management priorities aligning symptoms relief via medications identical those prescribed for other inflammatory conditions coupled with tailored physical therapy program aimed at posture improvement coupled with core strengthening exercises; persistent cases possibly requiring surgical decompression.

SKIN CONDITIONS

Skin, being the largest organ of the body, serves as the primary barrier between the internal systems and the external environment. A variety of skin conditions can affect this barrier function, leading to implications for massage practice.

Acne is a widely recognized condition characterized by clogged pores, pimples, and sometimes cysts. It's imperative for massage therapists to recognize that areas affected by severe acne should not be massaged, as this can cause irritation or spread infection.

Dermatitis encompasses various forms of skin inflammation, with symptoms including redness, swelling, itching, and blistering. Contact dermatitis arises from direct contact with an irritant or allergen and should be avoided during massage to prevent exacerbation or transfer of the allergen via the therapist's hands.

Eczema, or atopic dermatitis, is a chronic condition marked by dry, itchy patches of skin which can become inflamed and infected if scratched. When a client has eczema, it's essential to ensure that lotions or oils used during massage do not contain ingredients that could trigger a flare-up.

Psoriasis presents as areas of thickened, scaling skin due to an accelerated skin production process. These patches are often silver-white and can be found anywhere on the body. Understanding which areas are affected is vital since gentle techniques may be required for sensitive psoriatic plaques.

Fungal infections such as athlete's foot and ringworm create scaly patches on the skin or nails often accompanied by itching. These infections are contagious; therefore, clients with active fungal infections should not receive massage in the affected area.

Herpes simplex virus manifests through cold sores (HSV-1) or genital herpes (HSV-2). Given its infectious nature, clients with active cold sores or genital herpes outbreaks should not receive massage until lesions have fully healed.

Cellulitis is a bacterial infection presenting as redness and swelling on any part of the body. It occurs when bacteria enter through a break in the skin; this condition requires medical intervention and is a contraindication for massage due to its infectious potential.

Warts are growths caused by human papillomavirus (HPV) and appear as small, fleshy bumps on the skin. They are also contagious and therefore areas with warts should not be massaged directly.

Scabies infestation is due to mites burrowing into the top layer of skin causing intense itching. As scabies is highly contagious through direct contact, clients with an active infestation should not receive massage therapy.

Bruises or contusions denote injury below the surface resulting in blood collecting near the skin's surface—a sign of recent trauma. Massaging over a bruise can be painful for the client and potentially harmful; therefore, it should be avoided until fully healed.

Lastly, burns indicate tissue damage from excessive heat exposure ranging from sunburns to severe thermal burns. Fresh burns are absolute contraindications for massage as they need time to heal without additional pressure or manipulation which could aggravate them.

COMMUNICABLE DISEASES

A communicable disease can be caused by various pathogens, including bacteria, viruses, fungi, or parasites. These diseases may spread through direct contact with bodily fluids, airborne particles, contaminated surfaces, and vector organisms such as mosquitoes.

The body's first line of defense against these pathogens is the innate immune system, comprised of physical barriers such as skin and mucous membranes, chemical barriers like stomach acid, and cells that identify and destroy pathogens that enter the body. When these defenses are breached, the communicable disease takes root.

One well-known example of a bacterial communicable disease is tuberculosis (TB), which primarily impacts the lungs but can affect other parts of the body. It's characterized by a persistent cough with sputum, fever, night sweats, and weight loss. Another is streptococcal pharyngitis, often known as strep throat—a condition commonly treated with antibiotics to prevent complications like rheumatic fever.

Viral communicable diseases comprise a broad spectrum that includes the common cold, influenza, human immunodeficiency virus (HIV), which leads to acquired immune deficiency syndrome (AIDS), and emerging viruses like the severe acute respiratory syndrome coronavirus 2 (SARS-CoV-2), responsible for the disease COVID-19. These viral infections have varying levels of severity and impact on public health.

Fungal communicable diseases are less common but can include conditions such as ringworm or athlete's foot—dermatophytic infections of the skin caused by direct contact with fungal spores. These are typically not life-threatening but can cause discomfort and social stigma due to visible lesions on visible parts of the body.

Parasitic communicable diseases often conjure images of tropical maladies but are not confined to any single geographic area. Malaria is one such disease caused by Plasmodium parasites transmitted by the Anopheles mosquito. Its hallmark symptoms include fever, chills, and anemia. Others might include giardiasis or cryptosporidiosis—intestinal infections acquired through contaminated water or food sources.

Transmission of communicable diseases occurs via several mechanisms:

1. **Direct transmission:** Occurs when pathogens are passed through physical contact such as touching or kissing.
2. **Indirect transmission:** Happens when a person interacts with contaminated surfaces—a frequent occurrence with illnesses like norovirus.
3. **Droplet transmission:** Involves particles expelled during coughing or sneezing; it's how diseases like influenza spread.
4. **Airborne transmission:** Smaller particles remain in the air for extended periods and infect others over longer distances—as seen with tuberculosis.
5. **Vector-borne transmission:** Requires an intermediary organism. A prime example would be Lyme disease which is transmitted through tick bites.
6. **Vertical transmission:** Disease passed from mother to child during pregnancy, childbirth, or breastfeeding—syphilis and HIV are examples.

From a massage therapist's perspective—who may come in close contact with clients—it's critical to have a working knowledge of these diseases for several reasons:

1. To ensure proper sanitation practices to mitigate the spread within practice settings;
2. To recognize symptoms that may indicate a contraindication for massage;
3. To maintain personal health so as not to become both susceptible to infection and a vector for clients.

Preventative measures include rigorous hand hygiene—both hand washing with soap and water and using alcohol-based hand sanitizers; utilizing proper protective equipment like masks or gloves when necessary; ensuring clean linens for each client; sterilizing tools and equipment used during massage therapy; and maintaining current vaccination status where applicable.

Recognizing when massage therapy should be avoided is just as vital. Clients presenting with active signs or symptoms of communicable disease should be rescheduled for a future date when they're no longer contagious—for their welfare as well as yours and your other clients'.

CHAPTER 7
MASSAGE AND BODYWORK TECHNIQUES

SWEDISH MASSAGE

Swedish massage, a staple in Western spas and therapy practices, is heralded for its ability to promote relaxation, enhance circulation, and reduce muscle tension. This form of bodywork is not only a pleasurable experience but also a substantial component of holistic healing. It is foundational to most massage therapies and offers numerous benefits that reinforce the efficacy of manual bodywork in health and wellness.

Swedish massage emerged from the work of Per Henrik Ling, who developed the modality in the early 19th century. Combining his knowledge of gymnastics and his understanding of physiology, Ling sought to create a system that improved health through an interplay of exercise and massage. This technique employs five principal strokes:

1. **Effleurage:** This stroke forms the core of Swedish massage; characterized by long, gliding movements generally used at the beginning and end of a session. With effleurage, therapists use their palms, thumbs, or fingertips to apply light pressure that increases

blood flow and warms up the muscles. It's instrumental in introducing the client to the touch and establishing a nurturing connection.

2. **Petrissage:** Following effleurage, petrissage involves kneading the muscles with one hand or both hands, thumbs, or knuckles. This technique aims at deeper tissue structures with rhythmic lifting, rolling, and squeezing motions. By enhancing circulation to the muscle tissues, it helps release toxins and promotes deeper muscle relaxation.

3. **Friction:** In contrast to the calming movements of effleurage and petrissage, friction employs cross-fiber movements aimed at breaking down adhesions within soft tissues. These small, specific circles are often performed with fingers or thumbs over knots or strained areas providing targeted relief that re-establishes mobility between muscle fibers.

4. **Tapotement:** This stroke is like a symphony's crescendo played on the body's landscape. Comprising of fast-paced strikes such as hacking or cupping, tapotement energizes the body and stimulates nerve endings which may improve muscle tone and boost circulation.

5. **Vibration/shaking:** Concluding with vibrations or shaking techniques help reinforce the therapist's efforts throughout the session. By loosening up muscles through rapid back-and-forth movements either by hand or fingertips, this technique further assists in relaxation and releasing tension.

Beyond these strokes lies a philosophy rooted in caring touch and intent presence which therapists bring into each session. An effective Swedish massage addresses not just physical stress but also emotional well-being by using a supportive touch as a form of non-verbal communication that nurtures both body and mind.

Therapeutic benefits include improved sleep quality due to reduced stress levels; increased blood flow facilitating better oxygen supply throughout the body; enhanced immune system from lymph flow stimulation; reduction in physical pain through alleviating muscle tension; boosted mood via release of endorphins; aided detoxification processes; improved flexibility; decreased anxiety levels; among others.

In practice settings ranging from wellness spas to rehabilitation centers or private practices, Swedish massage adapts to diverse clientele needs - from athletes seeking restorative support to office workers bearing postural strain.

DEEP TISSUE MASSAGE

Deep tissue massage, a technique that realigns the deeper layers of muscles and connective tissues, is an essential tool for massage therapists, particularly for those preparing to take the MBLEX Exam. This type of massage is both a practical modality for treatment of chronic pain and a profound way to understand the body's structure and musculature at a deeper level.

The primary goal of deep tissue massage is to alleviate tension and reduce pain within the body's muscular system. To achieve this, therapists employ slower strokes and deeper pressure than in traditional Swedish massage, focusing on areas of tension and pain.

Before engaging in deep tissue techniques, it is crucial to have a comprehensive understanding of human anatomy. A therapist must be versed in the layers of muscle tissue, fascia, tendons, and ligaments they will be working with. Knowledge of common areas that harbor chronic tension, such as the neck, lower back, and shoulders is also important.

A typical deep tissue session begins much like other forms of massage – with an intention to relax the client. Starting with lighter pressure allows the superficial muscles to relax so that the therapist can gradually access deeper layers. Skipping this step can lead to unnecessary discomfort for the client and may result in resistance against the deeper pressure needed later in the session.

One technique employed during deep tissue massage is stripping. This involves applying deep, gliding pressure along the length of muscle fibers using thumbs, forearms, or elbows. The key here is slow movement; hurried strokes can induce more pain and work against muscle relaxation.

Another technique is friction, which involves applying pressure across the grain of a muscle to realign tissue fibers and release adhesions or "knots." Friction helps to promote movement within layers that may be stuck due to injury or chronic tension patterns.

A thorough knowledge of trigger points—areas where muscle knots may refer pain to other parts of the body—is vital for any therapist aiming to give an effective deep tissue massage. Addressing these trigger points can significantly decrease referred pain in clients and provides long-term relief from chronic conditions.

As with any type of therapy involving intense manipulation of muscles, there are contraindications for deep tissue massage that must be remembered. Clients with certain conditions such as acute injury, healing wounds, or inflammatory disorders like rheumatoid arthritis should avoid deep tissue techniques unless recommended by a healthcare provider.

In terms of preparation for the MBLEX Exam, understanding the principles behind deep tissue massage as well as when and how to apply them is critical. Therapists must also be familiar with potential reactions from clients during and following a deep tissue therapy session; these reactions might include temporary soreness or heightened emotions due to physical release from tight muscles.

Proper communication throughout a deep tissue session cannot be overstated. It's vital for therapists to check in frequently with clients about their comfort levels and adjust pressure accordingly. This type of feedback ensures safety and maximizes benefits while minimizing potential harm.

Additionally, self-care techniques should not be overlooked by therapists practicing deep tissue methods regularly. The physical exertion required can strain a practitioner's hands and wrists if proper body mechanics are not employed consistently. Therefore, understanding leverage techniques and using tools like forearm supports or special gloves are essential preventative measures.

Finally, for those studying for the MBLEX Exam—practice is essential. Not just in performing massages but also in studying anatomy, pathology, ethics and standards related practice management will play crucial roles in becoming proficient at delivering effective deep tissue massage treatments safely.

TRIGGER POINT THERAPY

Trigger points, often described as "knots" within the muscle fibers, can be sources of significant pain and discomfort for many individuals. Trigger points are typically characterized by palpable nodules in taut bands of muscles fibers. The exact mechanism is not fully understood but is believed to involve a dysfunctional motor endplate and an excessive release of acetylcholine leading to continuous muscle contraction. This constant contraction may result in local ischemia, which limits blood flow and oxygen to the tissue, perpetuating a cycle of pain and spasm.

Myofascial trigger points (MTrPs) can be classified into two categories: active and latent. Active MTrPs cause persistent pain that affects the quality of life, whereas latent MTrPs do not produce spontaneous pain but have the potential to become active under stress or muscular overload. It's critical for therapists to identify these distinctions during client assessments.

The goal of trigger point therapy is to disrupt this cycle by applying direct pressure on the affected areas to facilitate muscle relaxation and pain relief. The procedure usually follows several steps:

1. **Identifying Trigger Points:** A thorough examination is conducted by palpating the muscles to locate areas of tightness or tenderness indicative of trigger points.
2. **Pressure Application:** Once identified, consistent pressure is applied directly to these points with fingers, knuckles, or tools specifically designed for TPT.
3. **Duration:** Pressure is maintained generally for five to thirty seconds per trigger point or until a noticeable reduction in muscle tightness or patient discomfort is observed.
4. **Release and Stretch:** Following TPT, muscles should be gently stretched to improve range of motion and help prevent reformation of trigger points.

Trigger point therapy can be integrated into a massage session based on client need but should be performed within their comfort threshold. If performed too aggressively, TPT might heighten sympathetic arousal (the body's stress response), potentially worsening muscle tension and causing client distress.

Therapists should communicate with clients throughout the therapy session. Feedback helps determine pressure adequacy and discomfort level ensuring that TPT remains within tolerable limits while being effective.

Another critical consideration for MBLEX candidates is understanding contraindications for TPT. These include but are not limited to:

➢ Skin infections or open wounds at the site
➢ Recent surgery
➢ Bleeding disorders or clients on anticoagulant therapy
➢ Fractures or acute injuries
➢ Vascular disorders

Safe practice demands that therapists are mindful of these contraindications and proceed only when appropriate screening has been carried out.

In addition to manual techniques, certain complementary methods enhance TPT outcomes, such as:

1. Heat application beforehand to increase muscle pliability
2. Myofascial release techniques following TPT
3. Educating clients about proper ergonomics to reduce repetitive strain on muscles

4. Recommending exercises that strengthen opposing muscle groups

Research suggests that integrating these methodologies augments therapeutic results leading to more sustainable improvement in patient conditions.

Conclusively, understanding myofascial trigger points and their contribution to musculoskeletal pain reinforces why TPT is an effective treatment strategy taught in massage therapy curricula across educational platforms preparing students for practical examinations like the MBLEX. Crafting a holistic treatment plan that includes TPT requires comprehensive knowledge regarding anatomy, physiology, assessment skills, technique execution along with awareness regarding contra-actions subsequent administration.

It is essential for aspiring therapists to master concepts related to trigger point therapy as it represents both a prevalent concern amongst clients and palatially demonstrates a therapist's proficiency in addressing complex pain patterns innovatively and efficaciously. Preparation for certification exams should therefore heavily emphasize proficiency in these techniques as well as correlate scholarly theory with hands-on practice sessions that simulate real-world scenarios thereby equipping candidates with confidence and competence requisite for successful licensure attainment.

MYOFASCIAL RELEASE

Myofascial release is a therapeutic technique that addresses the discomfort associated with myofascial tissue—the tough membranes that wrap, connect, and support muscles. The fascia plays a significant role in muscle function and flexibility; when it's tight, it can lead to pain and restricted movement.

Fascia is composed of collagen fibers that cover and penetrate muscles, bones, nerves, arteries, and veins. Underneath the skin, it forms a structural support network that permeates throughout the body. Fascia's resiliency and pliability enable smooth gliding between tissues and help maintain structural integrity. However, factors such as overuse, injury, or surgery may tighten the fascia, causing myofascial restrictions which manifest as pain or reduced range of motion.

Myofascial release operates on several principles. It acknowledges that the body functions as a whole, and that tension in one area can affect movement elsewhere. This interconnectedness is why myofascial release can have far-reaching effects beyond the direct area being treated.

The technique involves applying gentle, sustained pressure into myofascial connective tissue restrictions. The pressure facilitates the release of tight fascia ('release') which promotes blood flow, restores range of motion, and reduces associated pain.

There are two primary methods for performing myofascial release: the direct method and the indirect method.

1. **The Direct Method:** In this approach, therapists apply forceful pressure into the fascia until they reach a restriction's depth. Then they maintain or increase pressure over time to facilitate elongation and release of the fascia.
2. **The Indirect Method:** Alternatively, therapists may apply less intense pressure in this approach. They gently stretch the fascia until reaching the tension barrier and hold it there for an extended period to allow for natural unwinding.

Both methods rely on feedback from the client's body to determine how much pressure to use and when release is occurring.

In clinical practice, myofascial release can be a stand-alone therapy or part of an integrated therapeutic approach. It helps with conditions such as chronic back pain, carpal tunnel syndrome, fibromyalgia, migraine headaches, and sports injuries—any situation where fascia may be implicated in pain or restricted movement.

It's crucial for massage therapists to evaluate each patient's unique situation before applying myofascial techniques. A thorough understanding of anatomy is imperative to identify those areas where myofascial release may be most beneficial.

While powerful on its own, myofascial release can be even more effective when integrated with complementary modalities like deep tissue massage or stretching exercises. Such combinations help address muscle tension at different depths and encourage comprehensive musculoskeletal health.

Therapists must keep several factors in mind when practicing myofascial release:

1. Always warm up muscles before beginning intensive work.
2. Remain sensitive to patients' pain thresholds—it should not be overly painful.
3. Maintain fluid communication with clients about what they are feeling during treatment.
4. Recognize signs indicating a need to adjust technique.
5. Pace sessions appropriately; changes in fascia do not happen instantly.

STRETCHING AND RANGE OF MOTION TECHNIQUES

Stretching refers to the deliberate lengthening of muscles to increase muscle flexibility and joint range of motion. Regular stretching is key to preventing the shortening and tightening of muscles that can lead to decreased flexibility, pain, and risk of injury. There are several types of stretches that may be utilized, including:

1. Static Stretching involves holding a stretch in a challenging yet comfortable position for a period, typically 15-30 seconds. It is effective at improving flexibility when performed consistently over time.
2. Dynamic Stretching consists of active movements that gently take your joints through their full range of motion. Unlike static stretching, dynamic stretches are not held in a position.
3. Ballistic Stretching uses bouncing movements to push the body beyond its normal range of motion. Due to its high risk of injury, this type is not commonly recommended.
4. Proprioceptive Neuromuscular Facilitation (PNF) involves both stretching and contracting the targeted muscle group and can be very effective for increasing ROM.

Stretching should always be performed on warmed-up muscles to avoid injury. It is essential not to overstretch, as this can lead to muscle tears.

Range of Motion (ROM) refers to the full movement potential of a joint, usually its range from flexion to extension or rotation. ROM exercises can be passive or active:

1. Passive ROM exercises involve moving joints through their range without exertion from the individual being stretched. These are helpful for maintaining mobility in individuals who cannot move their limbs independently due to conditions such as paralysis or severe weakness.
2. Active ROM exercises require the individual's muscular exertion to move their joints through their range. These exercises not only maintain joint flexibility but also help strengthen the muscles around the joint.

Incorporating regular stretching and ROM routines benefits everyone but holds special significance for those in therapeutic bodywork:

1. **Enhanced Flexibility:** Increased muscle flexibility allows for greater movement of personal joints during bodywork techniques. Flexible practitioners can perform their tasks with less risk of injury.

2. **Improved Client Outcomes:** By illustrating proper stretching and ROM exercises, therapists help clients manage pain, recover from injuries more efficiently, and improve overall quality of life.

3. **Injury Prevention:** Whether it's preparing your own body for work or assisting clients with their routines; incorporating these practices helps prevent injuries due to tight muscles or limited joint movement.

4. **Assessment Tools:** Therapists can use ROM assessments as a tool to measure client progress or inform treatment planning by clearly identifying restricted areas needing attention.

CHAPTER 8
PROFESSIONAL ETHICS AND STANDARDS

CODE OF ETHICS FOR MASSAGE THERAPISTS

The code of ethics serves as the backbone of professional integrity and client trust. It is essential in guiding therapists through the complexity of client interactions and ensuring that they conduct their practice keeping the clients' wellbeing as the central objective. It fosters a safe environment, upholds the industry standards, and safeguards both clients and therapists by delineating a clear framework within which ethical and professional decisions are made. Adherence to these guidelines reassures clients of their therapist's commitment to ethical practice, reinforces professional boundaries, and establishes a standard for accountability.

1. **Confidentiality and Privacy:** The first tenet of the Code of Ethics for massage therapists revolves around confidentiality and privacy. Clients entrust therapists with sensitive personal health information, expecting it to remain private. Respecting client confidentiality is not merely a best practice but also a legal requirement bound by HIPAA regulations in the United States. As a professional, one must ensure that all conversations, treatment details, and records are safeguarded with utmost discretion.

2. **Professional Boundaries:** The distinction between professional and personal relationships with clients is vital. Inherent in a massage therapist's work are intimacy and touch, which call for clear boundaries. Therapists must avoid dual relationships that could impair their professional judgment or increase the risk of exploitation. Sexual misconduct is an egregious violation of professional ethics and is absolutely forbidden. It is imperative to maintain respect, integrity, and professionalism at all times to create a safe environment for healing.

3. **Informed Consent:** Every treatment plan should begin with informed consent. Clients have the right to be fully informed about the techniques to be used as well as any potential risks involved in their treatment plan. Providing clients with this information allows them to make knowledgeable decisions about their body and therapy course. A comprehensive consent discussion encourages dialogue and reinforces client autonomy. Documenting that consent has been given is equally important for both client safety and practitioner accountability.

4. **Competence and Professionalism:** Maintaining competence through continuing education and adherence to industry standards assures clients receive high-quality care grounded in current practices and knowledge. Massage therapists must recognize their own skill limits, referring clients to other healthcare professionals when a client's needs are beyond what they can safely address. Presenting oneself professionally includes punctuality, cleanliness, proper attire, and preparation that respects the client's time and health.

5. **Respect for Diversity:** Therapists will encounter clients from diverse cultural backgrounds; sensitivity to these differences enriches the therapeutic relationship. Ethical practice involves providing equitable care without discrimination based on age, gender, race, ethnicity, national origin, sexual orientation, religion, disability or any other characteristic protected under applicable federal or state law.

6. **Commitment to Self-Care:** Finally, an often-overlooked component of ethical practice is self-care for practitioners themselves. To provide the best care for clients, therapists must be in good physical and mental health. They should engage in regular self-care routines that prevent burnout or physical injury which could compromise quality of service.

By adhering to this set of ethical principles - confidentiality and privacy; professional boundaries; informed consent; competency & professionalism; respect for diversity; commitment to self-care - massage therapists not only support ethical practice but elevate the standing of their profession within healthcare services.

SCOPE OF PRACTICE AND PROFESSIONALISM

Scope of Practice defines the boundaries within which therapists operate. It outlines the procedures, actions, and processes that a professional is permitted to undertake in keeping with the terms of their professional license. Knowing these limits protects therapists from legal issues and safeguards their careers by preventing practice outside of their competence, which could lead to physical harm to clients or ethical violations.

Moreover, Professionalism embodies the behaviors and attributes that are expected of massage therapists. This encompasses adherence to ethical standards, displaying respect for others, commitment to continued learning, accountability, and reliable customer service. It ensures that therapeutic relationships are built on trust and respect, which is vital for a successful practice.

In massage therapy, the Scope of Practice varies by region as each state or jurisdiction may have different regulations. Generally, it includes assessing clients' soft tissue condition, developing treatment plans, performing manipulations or techniques to promote health and well-being, maintaining client records accurately, and sharing information within the bounds of client confidentiality agreements.

It's imperative for therapists to understand local laws and regulations thoroughly. You'll need to be well-versed in contraindications for massage, understand when massage might not be beneficial or could cause harm – such as in cases of certain acute conditions, or where there might be skin infections or open wounds – and recognize situations where referral to another health professional is necessary.

Professionalism goes hand in hand with Scope of Practice; it governs how those guidelines are applied ethically. Respecting a client's boundaries and being mindful of personal bias ensures all treatments are delivered equitably. Moreover, setting clear boundaries about what is on offer in terms of treatment can avoid inappropriate requests from clients that fall outside the scope.

Keeping up with continuing education is another aspect of Professionalism in massage therapy. The field is constantly evolving with new treatments and methodologies emerging. As such, professionals must keep abreast of new techniques while remaining anchored in practices considered safe and effective.

Privacy is another critical domain within both professionalism and scope of practice parameters. Ensuring confidential handling of all client records not only protects privacy but complies with HIPAA regulations in the United States or equivalent standards internationally.

Additionally, maintaining an appropriate appearance, using proper draping techniques during sessions, punctuality, avoiding inappropriate language or behavior, managing business-related tasks diligently all reflect a professional demeanor which reinforces trust with clients.

CHAPTER 9
BUSINESS PRACTICES

STARTING AND MANAGING A MASSAGE THERAPY BUSINESS

As you head towards the MBLEX Exam and consider your future career, imagine the path of starting and managing your own massage therapy business. This challenging yet rewarding venture is not just about understanding the human body and mastering various massage techniques; it's also about entrepreneurship, branding, customer service, and financial management.

The first step in launching a massage therapy business is creating a robust business plan. This document outlines your vision for the business, services offered, market analysis, competitive landscape, marketing strategies, operational procedures, and financial projections. A solid plan will serve as a guideline for your business and is essential if you're seeking funding from investors or applying for loans.

Once your plan is in place, securing the necessary certifications and licenses is imperative. As a massage therapist, you'll need to comply with state regulations—which may include obtaining a license from a state board after passing exams like the MBLEX—and possibly additional local requirements.

Choosing the right location is crucial for a brick-and-mortar massage establishment. It should be accessible to clients, with enough foot traffic to encourage walk-in appointments yet serene enough to maintain a relaxing atmosphere. Consider rent costs, zoning laws, renovation expenses, and the proximity to complementary businesses when deciding on your location.

Investing in high-quality equipment and supplies is the next step. This includes massage tables or chairs, linens, oils or lotions, towels, and other necessary items that ensure client comfort and enhance their therapeutic experience. Ergonomic furniture for you is also essential to prevent practitioner injury over time.

Hiring skilled staff can make or break your business. Depending on the size of your venture at the outset, this might mean hiring other massage therapists or receptionists. Look for individuals who are not only technically proficient but who also embody strong interpersonal skills since they'll contribute significantly to the overall customer experience.

Developing an effective marketing strategy is paramount in attracting clients. Your strategy might combine online marketing (such as social media campaigns or search engine optimization) with traditional methods (like flyers and community networking). Building a strong brand for your massage therapy business helps differentiate it from competitors—a unique logo and service philosophy can go a long way.

To manage client relationships effectively requires an organized booking system—for scheduling appointments to managing cancellations—and a follow-up method to keep regular clients engaged and attract new ones through their referrals. Implementing customer relationship management (CRM) software can aid greatly in this facet of management.

Financial management entails establishing clear pricing models that reflect both the value provided to clients and cover operational costs while remaining competitive within your market segment. Keeping accurate records of all transactions helps in monitoring cash flow. It's wise to use accounting software or hire an accountant who's familiar with small businesses' needs.

Risk management is another aspect often overlooked by new entrepreneurs. Ensure that you have adequate insurance coverage—from property insurance for your office space to professional liability insurance should any mishaps occur during treatment sessions.

Lastly but importantly: Professional Development. Stay updated with industry trends; continue learning new modalities of massage therapy which can expand services offered to clients—this facilitates growth both personally and financially as you adapt to an evolving marketplace.

Starting and managing a successful massage therapy business requires balancing technical skills with savvy business acumen. Alongside continuous self-improvement as a therapist, fostering excellent customer service practices will foster fruitful client relationships that are foundational for any successful service-oriented enterprise.

By charting out your course diligently through planning, legal adherence, focusing on client needs while developing smart operational procedures and branding strategies—your massage therapy practice will not only pass the MBLEX but stand ready to thrive in today's competitive wellness industry.

CLIENT COMMUNICATION AND DOCUMENTATION

Communication with clients sets the stage for a successful therapeutic relationship. It begins with the initial intake where you gather crucial health history and understand their present concerns and wellness goals. During this interview process, practice active listening to accurately capture their needs. This does not merely involve hearing their words but also paying close attention to non-verbal cues such as body language, facial expressions, and tone, which can offer additional insights into their state of wellbeing.

Always explain your proposed treatment plan clearly, detailing the techniques you intend to use and their benefits. Transparency about what your client can expect during the session fosters trust and comfort. Moreover, it is crucial to obtain informed consent before proceeding with any massage therapy services. This means that the client should be aware of potential risks and agree to the treatment voluntarily – a fundamental ethical principle in healthcare provision.

Throughout the session, continue effective communication by checking in with your client about pressure levels and comfort. Your intuitive skills will also be at play here; sensitize yourself to non-verbal signals that may indicate discomfort or distress. After the session, debrief with your client by discussing their experience and any follow-up care recommendations.

Proper documentation is another critical aspect of your role as a massage therapist. Accurate records not only provide a history of client sessions for future reference but also serve as legal documents that protect both you and your client. Each interaction should be recorded in detail within the client's file including:

1. Personal information gathered during the initial interview.
2. A clear account of their reported symptoms and health history.
3. Treatment goals set in collaboration with the client.

4. Plans for treatment including types of massage techniques used.

5. The response to treatment, as observed during and after the session.

6. Updates on any changes in health status or goals.

7. Informed consent for each treatment provided.

Ensure that all documentation follows HIPAA guidelines or equivalent privacy laws applicable in your locale for protecting sensitive patient information.

Effective use of SOAP notes – which stands for Subjective, Objective, Assessment, and Plan – will ensure you keep structured records that communicate essential information succinctly. 'Subjective' covers what the client tells you about their condition; 'Objective' involves what you observe; 'Assessment' relates to your professional evaluation; and 'Plan' outlines the continuing treatment strategy.

Be timely with your documentation – promptly recording information after each session when details are fresh in your mind minimizes errors or omissions. Use clear language free from ambiguity so that anyone reviewing the notes can understand them without difficulty.

Lastly, consider ongoing education regarding professional communication and record-keeping best practices as laws, standards, and technologies evolve over time. Remember: every word exchanged with a client is an opportunity to heal – both verbally through empathy and caring – or literally through your hands-on work guided by accurate record-keeping on all facets of their treatment journey.

CHAPTER 10
CLIENT ASSESSMENT AND TREATMENT PLANNING

ASSESSING CLIENT NEEDS

Prior to any physical examination or hands-on therapy, the initial step in assessing client needs is through a thorough intake process. An intake form should gather comprehensive information on a client's medical history, current conditions, medications, lifestyle factors, and past experiences with massage. However, it goes beyond just gathering data; it requires active listening and empathy to truly understand their perspective and health-related goals.

Once you have gathered information through the intake process, the next vital step is conducting a verbal interview. This allows you to clarify any points on the intake form and probe deeper into areas that require more detail. Your questions should aim to uncover not just what clients think they need, but also needs they may not be consciously aware of.

After an insightful interview, observing visual cues becomes a tool of great importance. Clients may not always be able to articulate their needs or discomforts perfectly. It is through observation that a therapist can identify signs of stress, pain, or discomfort manifesting as physical attributes such as postural imbalances or movement restrictions.

The verbal and visual assessment should seamlessly transition into palpation techniques during the session's initial minutes. As you apply your touch, be attentive to muscular tension, texture changes in tissues, and the client's reaction to pressure. These tactile cues will guide your massage strategies and adjust them according to the feedback provided by the client's body.

It is equally essential to continuously communicate with your client throughout the session. This interactive approach ensures that you are aligned with the client's comfort levels and expectations. Enabling such dialogue empowers clients to take an active role in their healing process while helping you cater your techniques for maximum benefit.

The concept of contraindications must not be overlooked when assessing client needs. Recognizing conditions that require modification or avoidance of certain techniques will protect both client and therapist from potential harm. As part of your MBLEX preparation, understanding these contraindications in depth is imperative for safe practice.

Considering emotional and psychological factors during assessment is also necessary since mental health significantly influences physical well-being. Clients may carry emotional stress in their bodies that manifests as muscular tension or imbalances; recognizing this link can profoundly affect your treatment plan choices.

Professionalism establishes clear boundaries while showing genuine care shapes a trust-filled therapist-client relationship. It encourages honest communication regarding pain thresholds, treatment preferences, and desired outcomes so that clients feel heard and valued.

Every client presents a unique set of circumstances; therefore, adapting individualized treatment plans is key. From developing targeted goals based on assessments to deciding on modalities best suited for achieving those goals—flexibility in planning upholds quality services tailored to individual needs. Finally, conducting post-session evaluations allows therapists to measure effectiveness against objectives set during planning and provides an opportunity for feedback which can refine future sessions.

DEVELOPING A TREATMENT PLAN

Developing a treatment plan serves as a blueprint that guides the massage therapist through a client's sessions, ensuring each move and technique is purposeful and directed toward the client's goals. Treatment plans are vital because they provide structure and direction, facilitate measurable outcomes, and increase the efficacy of therapy. The planning process takes into account the client's health history, current condition, and personal preferences, all while keeping safety at the forefront.

Creating an individualized treatment plan helps ensure success by integrating assessment findings with knowledge of anatomy, physiology, pathology, and massage techniques. It allows therapists to set realistic goals and time frames for achieving them. A well-formulated treatment plan enhances therapist-client communication by clearly outlining expectations, facilitating participation in one's own healing process, and fostering trust. Ultimately, this systematic approach is fundamental for professional credibility and enhances the therapist's ability to make informed decisions that support client wellness and recovery.

When transitioning into creating an effective treatment plan, there are several key elements a massage therapist must consider:

1. **Client Assessment:** Every treatment plan should start with a comprehensive client assessment. This includes reviewing their health history forms, understanding their current level of pain or discomfort, range of motion limitations or other functional impairments, as well as any relevant psychological factors such as stress levels which might impact their physical wellbeing.

2. **Goal Setting:** Establish clear short-term and long-term goals that are SMART (Specific, Measurable, Achievable, Relevant, Time-bound). These goals should be agreed upon with the client to ensure they are motivated to pursue them through therapeutic intervention.

3. **Technique Selection and Sequencing:** Based on the assessment results and goals set forth in collaboration with the client, select appropriate massage techniques like Swedish massage for relaxation or trigger point therapy for specific pain relief. Sequence these techniques in a logical manner that respects tissue adaptability and avoids over-treatment.

4. **Treatment Adaptability:** Effective treatment plans are adaptable to changes in the client's condition over time. Modify techniques or strategies if certain movements elicit discomfort or if there's an unforeseen change in the client's health status.

5. **Documentation:** Detailed documentation after every session provides a record of progress over time which is crucial both for legal and professional reasons. It can also inform future revisions to the treatment plan as needed.

6. **Client Education:** Take time within sessions to educate clients on self-care strategies such as stretching, strengthening exercises or relaxation methods that can enhance their progress outside of massage appointments.

7. **Reassessment:** Regular reassessment will determine if the objectives are being met or need revision. Use reassessment data to make clinical decisions about continuing with your current course of action or altering your approach.

8. **Ethical Considerations:** At all times ensure that your treatment plan adheres to ethical standards and only includes approaches for which you're qualified and that fit within the scope of practice.

Working through these steps systematically increases the likelihood that you will be able to facilitate significant improvements in your clients' health outcomes—a centerpiece for any massage therapy professional aiming at overarching wellness goals.

When engaging in developing a treatment plan as part of MBLEX prep or actual practice, visualize it not only as a roadmap but also as a living document that morphs alongside your clients' evolving needs—and one that underscores your commitment to providing thoughtful, high-grade care grounded in industry best practices.

CHAPTER 11
PRACTICE EXAMS

ANATOMY AND PHYSIOLOGY (11%)

1. Which system is responsible for transporting nutrients, oxygen, and waste throughout the body?

   a) Digestive System
   b) Nervous System
   c) Circulatory System
   d) Endocrine System

2. What type of tissue is specialized for contraction and generating force?

   a) Epithelial tissue
   b) Connective tissue
   c) Muscle tissue
   d) Nervous tissue

3. Which component of the nervous system controls voluntary muscle movements?

   a) Autonomic Nervous System
   b) Somatic Nervous System
   c) Sympathetic Nervous System

d) Parasympathetic Nervous System

4. Osteoblasts are cells that are primarily involved in:

  a) Breaking down bone tissue.
  b) Forming new bone tissue.
  c) Producing red blood cells.
  d) Repairing nervous tissue.

5. Which layer of the skin contains sweat glands, hair follicles, and sebaceous glands?

  a) Epidermis
  b) Dermis
  c) Hypodermis
  d) Stratum corneum

6. The contraction of which muscle will decrease the volume of the thoracic cavity during expiration?

  a) Diaphragm
  b) External intercostal muscles
  c) Internal intercostal muscles
  d) Scalene muscles

7. The exchange of oxygen and carbon dioxide occurs in which part of the respiratory system?

  a) Trachea
  b) Bronchi
  c) Bronchioles
  d) Alveoli

8. In a process known as "depolarization," which ion flows into a neuron to generate an action potential?

  a) Potassium (K+)
  b) Calcium (Ca2+)
  c) Sodium (Na+)
  d) Chloride (Cl-)

9. The humoral immune response is primarily mediated by:

  a) T-cells

b) B-cells

c) Neutrophils

d) Macrophages

10. Which type of connective tissue connects muscles to bones?

a) Ligaments

b) Tendons

c) Fascia

d) Cartilage

11. In terms of energetic anatomy, what corresponds to the energy center located at the throat area?

a) Root Chakra

b) Sacral Chakra

c) Solar Plexus Chakra

d) Throat Chakra

KINESIOLOGY (12%)

12. Which muscle contraction occurs when the muscle shortens as it develops tension?

   a) Isometric
   b) Eccentric
   c) Concentric
   d) Isokinetic

13. Which type of muscle fiber is characterized by rapid force production and fast fatigue?

   a) Type I fibers
   b) Type IIa fibers
   c) Type IIb fibers
   d) Intermediate fibers

14. What is the role of Golgi tendon organs in proprioception?

   a) Detect changes in muscle length
   b) Detect changes in muscular tension
   c) Control voluntary movements
   d) Detect changes in temperature within muscles

15. What is the origin of the deltoid muscle?

   a) Clavicle and scapula
   b) Humerus and radius
   c) Femur and tibia
   d) Ilium and sacrum

16. During a bicep curl, which type of lever is primarily being used at the elbow joint?

   a) First-class lever
   b) Second-class lever
   c) Third-class lever
   d) Fourth-class lever

17. Which term best describes a muscles' action that moves away from the midline of the body?

   a) Abduction
   b) Adduction
   c) Flexion

d) Extension

18. Which proprioceptors are sensitive to change in length and the rate of change within muscles?

a) Ruffini endings
b) Muscle spindles
c) Pacinian corpuscles
d) Merkel discs

19. What is known as the range through which a joint can be moved, usually its range of flexion and extension?

a) Torque range
b) Tension range
c) Range of motion (ROM)
d) Reach range

20. Which type of joint allows for the widest range of motion?

a) Hinge joint
b) Pivot joint
c) Ball-and-socket joint
d) Saddle joint

21. When discussing muscle attachments, what is the 'origin' specifically referring to?

a) The site where nervous input stimulates muscle contraction
b) The end that typically remains stationary during contraction
c) The part that directly receives blood supply
d) The midpoint between agonist and antagonist muscles

22. What is an example of a voluntary muscle action?

a) Heart beating
b) Diaphragm contracting for breathing
c) Reflex arc actions
d) Deciding to walk

23. Range of motion (ROM) exercises aim primarily at improving what aspect of joint health?

a) Synovial fluid distribution

b) Fibrous connective tissue elasticity

c) Muscular strength

d) Joint flexibility

PATHOLOGY, SPECIAL POPULATIONS, CONTRAINDICATIONS, AND AREAS OF CAUTION (14%)

24. Which of the following is considered a systemic contraindication for massage?

   a) Muscle soreness

   b) Local inflammation

   c) Fever

   d) Bruise

25. What pathological condition is characterized by the thickening and hardening of arterial walls?

   a) Atherosclerosis

   b) Myalgia

   c) Atrophy

   d) Tendonitis

26. In which of these conditions should massage therapy be avoided altogether?

   a) Diabetes, with controlled blood sugar

   b) Chronic muscle tension

   c) Immediately after surgery

   d) Osteoarthritis

27. Which condition may benefit from massage therapy but requires a physician's approval before treatment?

   a) High blood pressure

   b) Recent fracture

   c) Ankylosing spondylitis

   d) Infectious skin disease

28. Lymphedema refers to:

   a) Wasting away of muscle tissue due to lack of use

   b) Swelling due to accumulation of lymph fluid in tissues

   c) Inflammation of a lymph node

   d) Chronic muscle pain without inflammation

29. What is oncology massage?

    a) Massage for clients with fibromyalgia

    b) Massage tailored for individuals with cancer histories

    c) Massage using stones heated by oncological processes

    d) Specialized massage techniques for people suffering from chronic fatigue syndrome

30. When massaging a client with diabetes, which of the following areas should you approach with Caution?

    a) Feet and lower legs

    b) Upper back

    c) Shoulders

    d) Forearms

31. Why is it important to avoid deep massage strokes over the abdomen of a pregnant client?

    a) To prevent induction of labor

    b) It can lead to nausea

    c) To avoid disruption to fetal development

    d) All of the above

32. A client who recently had surgery is looking to receive a massage. When should massage be avoided?

    a) 2 weeks after surgery

    b) 24 hours after surgery

    c) Until cleared by a physician

    d) Massage is always safe post-surgery

33. Which class of medication is important to be aware of due to its blood-thinning properties that could lead to bruising?

    a) Antihistamines

    b) Antibiotics

    c) Anticoagulants

    d) Antidepressants

34. In clients with varicose veins, massage therapists should:

a) Massage directly over the varicosities with firm pressure.

b) Avoid massaging the affected areas.

c) Only use tapotement techniques on the area.

d) Perform deep tissue massage around the site.

35. Which population should not receive deep tissue massage?

a) Athletes after training sessions.

b) Clients suffering from osteoporosis.

c) Clients who experience muscle soreness.

d) Clients without chronic injuries.

36. What precaution must be taken when massaging a client taking corticosteroids?

a) Avoiding deep pressure techniques

b) Using only cold therapy

c) Implementing vigorous strokes

d) Applying heat for an extended time

37. For a client undergoing chemotherapy, what is an important consideration for massage therapy?

a) Use stronger pressure for stimulation purposes.

b) Avoid long sessions as they may become overstimulated.

c) Maintain firm, sustained strokes throughout the session.

d) Avoid massage due to potential lymphedema and fragility concerns.

BENEFITS AND PHYSIOLOGICAL EFFECTS OF TECHNIQUES THAT MANIPULATE SOFT TISSUE (15%)

38. Which of the following is a physiological effect of soft tissue manipulation?

   a) Slowed heart rate
   b) Decrease in blood circulation
   c) Increased pain sensation
   d) Reduction in immune system function

39. Touch can convey warmth, safety, and comfort due to its ability to:

   a) Release endorphins
   b) Stimulate the adrenal glands
   c) Increase muscle tension
   d) Relax the digestive system

40. For an elderly client with arthritis, what benefit might soft tissue manipulation provide?

   a) Decreased joint flexibility
   b) Increased stiffness and swelling
   c) Improved range of motion
   d) Worsened chronic pain

41. Which system is responsible for the 'relaxation response' during soft tissue manipulation?

   a) Respiratory system
   b) Sympathetic nervous system
   c) Parasympathetic nervous system
   d) Lymphatic system

42. Athletes may benefit from soft tissue manipulation primarily because it helps:

   a) Decrease performance levels
   b) Improve cardiovascular health
   c) Reduce recovery time after an injury
   d) Increase risk of injury

43. In terms of psychological aspects, soft tissue manipulation helps reduce stress by:

   a) Increasing cortisol production

b) Lowering sympathetic nervous activity

c) Intensifying alertness

d) Elevating blood pressure

44. How does soft tissue manipulation positively affect the integumentary system?

a) By decreasing skin elasticity

b) By reducing the supply of oxygen and nutrients to skin cells

c) By stimulating blood flow to the area, which nourishes skin cells

d) By promoting hair loss

45. Pregnant women may get relief from sore and tense muscles through soft tissue manipulation because it:

a) Reduces levels of neurotransmitters associated with pain sensation

b) Increases discomfort due to heightened sensitivity during pregnancy

c) Elevates blood pressure restricting blood flow to extremities

d) Optimizes joint alignment by tightening ligaments

46. Soft tissue manipulation has been shown to have various benefits during post-operative care, such as:

a) Increasing scar tissue formation

b) Reducing edema and improving lymphatic flow

c) Causing re-injury to the affected area

d) Inhibiting wound healing processes

47. Which of the following is a common physiological effect of soft tissue manipulation?

a) Decrease in blood circulation

b) Increase in local inflammation

c) Reduction in muscle tension

d) Impairment of skin elasticity

48. How does the application of cold therapy affect soft tissue?

a) It increases tissue extensibility.

b) It reduces the metabolic rate of tissues.

c) It causes vasodilation.

d) It increases nutrient flow to the affected area.

49. Which technique involves a gentle, rhythmic pumping action on the body's soft tissues and is primarily aimed at stimulating the lymphatic system?

a) Shiatsu

b) Myofascial release

c) Manual lymphatic drainage

d) Trigger point therapy

50. What benefit does myofascial release aim to achieve through manipulation of soft tissue?

a) Improvement in muscular strength

b) Decrease in nerve compression

c) Enhancement of skin tone

d) Shortening of muscle fibers

51. Which modality uses heated stones placed on specific points on the body to relax muscles?

a) Aromatherapy massage

b) Reflexology

c) Hot stone massage

d) Thai massage

52. How does hot application differ from cold application in terms of blood vessel response?

a) Hot application results in vasoconstriction, while cold causes vasodilation.

b) Both hot and cold applications cause vasodilation.

c) Hot application causes vasodilation, while cold results in vasoconstriction.

d) Both hot and cold applications result in vasoconstriction.

53. When considering contraindications for certain modalities that manipulate soft tissue, which factor is important for a therapist to consider prior to applying heat or cold treatments?

a) The client's preference for heat or cold sensations

b) The presence of acute or chronic injuries

c) The time duration since injury onset only

d) The client's level of physical activity

CLIENT ASSESSMENT, REASSESSMENT, AND TREATMENT PLAN FORMULATION (17%)

54. When organizing a session for a new client's massage therapy, what is the first step taken by the therapist?

a) Conduct a physical examination

b) Prepare the massage table with necessary supplies

c) Review the written data provided by the client

d) Begin the massage immediately to assess tissue response

55. What is an essential component of a client's initial assessment in massage therapy?

a) Discussing payment options

b) Evaluating range of motion and posture

c) Suggesting dietary changes

d) Recommending exercise routines

56. During reassessment, a client reports reduced pain and increased mobility since their last session. What should this indicate to a therapist?

a) The previous treatment plan needs to be continued without change.

b) The current treatment plan may require adjustments based on improvement.

c) Massage therapy is no longer necessary.

d) The focus should shift entirely to relaxation techniques.

57. Why is it important for therapists to collect written data from clients before commencing treatment?

a) It fulfills insurance requirements only.

b) It helps customize the session according to client needs.

c) It allows therapists to avoid any physical assessment.

d) It gives insight into what aromatherapy scents the client prefers.

58. A thorough client consultation before starting massage therapy primarily ensures:

a) A quick start to therapy sessions without proper planning

b) Identification of contraindications for certain techniques or modalities

c) Standardization of all massages regardless of individual differences

d) Application of the most pressure possible for maximum effect

59. In facilitating treatment plan formulation, goal setting with the client is vital because it:

    a) Minimizes legal liability for the therapist alone

    b) Helps guide the types of massage techniques and therapies used

    c) Ensures that sessions are as short as possible

    d) Guarantees permanent resolution of all symptoms

60. When should a reassessment typically occur in a series of massage therapy sessions?

    a) Only when a client complains about discomfort

    b) At regular intervals throughout the treatment series

    c) Solely at the end of a package of sessions

    d) Whenever there is a full moon

61. Which type of information would NOT typically be collected from a written intake form provided by clients?

    a) Current stress levels

    b) Previous surgeries and medical history

    c) Daily caloric intake

    d) Medications being taken

62. When visually assessing a client's posture, what is a key indicator of possible kyphosis?

    a) Exaggerated lumbar curve

    b) Rounded shoulders and a forward head position

    c) Knees hyperextended

    d) Flattening of the thoracic curve

63. During palpation, you notice that a muscle feels unusually dense and taut. This could indicate:

    a) Muscle atrophy

    b) A muscle spasm

    c) Myxedema

    d) Increased blood flow

64. If a client is unable to fully abduct their arm at the shoulder joint, this limitation in range of motion may be due to:

a) Scapular winging

b) Frozen shoulder

c) Bursitis in the hip

d) A sprained ankle

65. In clinical reasoning, why would a massage therapist refer a client to another healthcare professional?

a) The client's condition does not fall within the therapist's scope of practice

b) The client asks about nutritional advice

c) The therapist has fully booked appointments

d) The client prefers a different style of massage

66. What is the primary intent of reassessing a client during subsequent visits?

a) To adjust the treatment plan if needed based on changes in condition or progress

b) To comply with insurance requirements

c) To charge additional fees for assessment procedures

d) To lengthen the duration of therapy

67. When assessing clients using palpation, what would indicate an area of inflammation?

a) Increased local temperature

b) Presence of adhesions

c) Decreased tissue density

d) Cooler sensation compared to surrounding areas

68. Observing which of these factors would be least useful when conducting an overall general assessment of a client?

a) Skin color and texture

b) Client's medical history

c) Current weather conditions

d) Symmetry or asymmetry in body structure

69. How might checking a client's range of motion contribute to treatment plan formulation?

a) It can reveal areas with reduced movement that may benefit from targeted techniques.

b) It ensures legal protection for the therapist against malpractice.

c) It provides information about clients' exercise habits.

d) It offers insights into clients' dietary deficiencies.

ETHICS, LAWS, AND BOUNDARIES IN MASSAGE THERAPY (16%)

70. What does having ethical behavior in massage therapy practice primarily ensure?

    a) Higher profit margins

    b) Client retention

    c) Protection of the client's well-being

    d) More efficient treatment plans

71. Why are boundaries important in a professional massage therapy environment?

    a) To protect the therapist's personal space

    b) To ensure clear professional roles are maintained

    c) To create a hierarchical structure within the clinic

    d) To encourage personal relationships with clients

72. Which action is considered a code of ethics violation in massage therapy?

    a) Refusing service due to discrimination

    b) Requiring payment at time of service

    c) Providing educational information to a client

    d) Keeping accurate client treatment records

73. How can a therapeutic relationship be best defined?

    a) A friendship between the therapist and client

    b) An ongoing social interaction outside of scheduled sessions

    c) A professional alliance geared toward meeting the client's therapeutic goals

    d) A casual acquaintance that may lead to social activities

74. What is an example of a dual relationship in massage therapy?

    a) Providing therapy to someone in your immediate family.

    b) Attending professional seminars with colleagues.

    c) Upgrading your clinic's massage tables.

    d) Networking at industry events for job opportunities.

75. Which ethical foundation is focused on doing good or what is beneficial for a client?

    a) Beneficence

b) Justice

c) Autonomy

d) Nonmaleficence

76. What should you do if you realize a session may trigger emotional distress for a client?

a) Continue without adjusting your technique.

b) Dismiss their reaction as unimportant.

c) Redirect them to talk about happier topics.

d) Stop treatment and offer support or referrals if necessary.

77. What should a massage therapist do if they find themselves entering into an unethical dual relationship with a client?

a) Engage fully in this new role as long as it feels comfortable.

b) Set clear boundaries or refer to another therapist if necessary.

c) Discuss it during sessions to get consensus from the client.

d) Ignore it since intentions are not harmful.

78. What should a massage therapist do if a client suggests sexual services?

a) Report the incident to their supervisor

b) Ignore the comment and continue the massage

c) Politely decline and inform the client that this is outside the scope of practice

d) End the session and document the incident in the client's record

79. Under which circumstance can a massage therapist breach client confidentiality?

a) When talking about a case with another therapist for advice

b) When ordered by a court of law

c) When discussing the treatment with friends or family

d) Confidentiality should never be breached under any circumstances

80. Which of these statements is outside a massage therapist's scope of practice?

a) Suggesting relaxation techniques to a client

b) Prescribing medication to relieve pain

c) Educating a client about stress management

d) Providing advice on postural improvements

81. How should massage therapists handle receiving gifts from clients that could potentially affect impartiality?

a) Accept all gifts graciously to avoid offending clients

b) Politely decline all gifts from clients

c) Only accept gifts if they are under a certain monetary value

d) Accept gifts only during the holiday season

82. What constitutes effective communication with a client during an initial consultation?

a) Providing detailed explanations of all potential therapies

b) Ensuring that medical jargon is used to establish professionalism

c) Listening intently to the client's concerns and asking relevant questions

d) Speaking continuously so that all information is conveyed quickly

83. A massage therapist accidentally views another patient's health information while updating records. What is the appropriate action?

a) Do nothing unless it happens repeatedly

b) Report it to their supervisor as an incidental exposure

c) Share it only if it seems relevant for public interest

d) Discuss it with other colleagues for their opinion on it

84. Which principle emphasizes that a therapist should do good and provide benefit in therapeutic relationships?

a) Autonomy

b) Justice

c) Beneficence

d) Fidelity

85. What action should be taken if a massage therapist realizes they have overbooked clients due to administrative error?

a) Proceed with shorter sessions for each client without notice

b) Postpone all appointments by one day

c) Communicate with impacted clients offering acceptable alternatives

d) Cancel only new client appointments as they are less likely to complain

GUIDELINES FOR PROFESSIONAL PRACTICE (15%)

86. What is the first step in proper sanitization of massage equipment?

   a) Rinsing with water
   b) Applying an EPA-registered disinfectant
   c) Wiping with a clean cloth
   d) Pre-cleaning with soap and water

87. How often should the headrest cover of a massage table be changed?

   a) After each client
   b) Once a day
   c) Every week
   d) Twice a day

88. Which of the following is NOT required to maintain cleanliness in a massage therapy room?

   a) Disinfecting the massage table after every use
   b) Changing linens between clients
   c) Using a fresh bottle of massage oil for every session
   d) Disposing of any single-use items immediately after use

89. When should a massage therapist wash their hands?

   a) Only before starting the massage session
   b) Only after finishing the massage session
   c) Before eating or drinking anything
   d) Both A and B

90. What is the minimum recommended time for leaving an EPA-registered disinfectant on a surface to ensure proper sanitization?

   a) 30 seconds
   b) 1 minute
   c) 5 minutes
   d) 10 minutes

91. If a client has a skin condition, what is the BEST course of action regarding the use of massage linens?

   a) Proceed with using common linens as usual
   b) Use disposable linens and wear gloves during the session

c) Reschedule the appointment until the condition clears

d) Apply extra disinfectant after the session

92. Which temperature setting is recommended when laundering used linens from massage therapy sessions?

a) Cold water setting

b) Warm water setting

c) Hot water setting

d) Any temperature as long as a strong detergent is used

93. What safety practice should be followed when using electrical equipment such as heating pads or warm towel cabinets in a massage therapy session?

a) Use power strips instead of direct wall outlets.

b) Ensure all equipment is properly grounded.

c) Only use equipment that produces a light buzzing sound.

d) Use extension cords regularly to keep cables away from clients.

94. Which of the following is a recommended self-care practice for massage therapists to prevent burnout?

a) Taking additional part-time work outside of massage therapy

b) Scheduling massages back-to-back without breaks

c) Implementing regular exercise and healthy eating into their routine

d) Limiting sleep to increase the number of client appointments

95. What is the primary purpose of draping techniques during a massage session?

a) To keep the client warm and comfortable

b) To advertise the massage therapist's services

c) To use as much linen as possible for hygiene reasons

d) To restrict the client's movement on the table

96. Effective communication in a massage therapy business should include:

a) Only discussions about the therapist's personal life to build rapport

b) Use of technical jargon to demonstrate knowledge

c) Clear, professional discussion regarding treatment plans, goals, and consent

d) Avoiding any conversation about a client's treatment progress

97. How often should a massage therapist review their business plan?

a) Once when they first write it and then never again.

b) Every 5 years.

c) Annually, or as needed to adjust for changes in their business.

d) Only when advised by a financial advisor.

98. In healthcare terminology, 'SOAP notes' stand for subjective, objective, assessment, and what?

a) Planning

b) Prescription

c) Procedure

d) Performance

99. What is meant by 'scope of practice' in the context of massage therapy?

a) The décor style of one's practice setting.

b) The legal boundaries defining what services can be provided.

c) The pricing structure for different types of massages.

d) The geographic location where one can practice legally.

100. Which insurance type is most important for a massage therapist to have?

a) Health insurance only for themselves.

b) Automobile insurance because therapists may need to travel.

c) Liability insurance to protect against potential claims related to their practice.

d) Life insurance solely for personal coverage.

ANSWER KEYS AND EXPLANATIONS

1. C: The circulatory system, consisting of the heart, blood vessels, and blood, is responsible for the transportation of nutrients, oxygen, and waste products.

2. C: Muscle tissue is specialized to contract and produce movement or generate force in the body.

3. B: The somatic nervous system controls voluntary movements of skeletal muscles.

4. B: Osteoblasts are cells that secrete the matrix for bone formation and are involved in bone growth and repair.

5. B: The dermis is the middle layer of the skin that contains sweat glands, hair follicles, and sebaceous (oil) glands.

6. C: The internal intercostal muscles contract during forced expiration to depress the ribs and decrease thoracic volume.

7. D: Alveoli are small sacs within the lungs where gas exchange between air and blood takes place.

8. C: Sodium ions (Na+) flow into a neuron during depolarization to generate an action potential.

9. B: B-cells are responsible for producing antibodies in the humoral immune response against pathogens.

10. B: Tendons are fibrous connective tissues that attach muscle to bone, transferring forces produced by muscle contractions to move bones.

11. D: In energetic anatomy, the throat chakra is believed to be located at the throat area and is associated with communication and self-expression.

12. C: Concentric contractions involve the shortening of a muscle as it develops tension and contracts against resistance.

13. C: Type IIb fibers, also known as fast-twitch or white fibers, are known for their rapid force production and quicker fatigue rates compared to other fiber types.

14. B: Golgi tendon organs are proprioceptors that track changes in the tension of muscles, helping to prevent injury from overloading.

15. A: The deltoid muscle originates from the lateral third of the clavicle, acromion, and spine of the scapula.

16. C: The human body primarily uses third-class levers, where the effort is between the fulcrum (joint) and the load (weight in hand during a curl).

17. A: Abduction refers to movements that take limbs away from the midline or center of the body.

18. B: Muscle spindles are sensory receptors within muscles that respond to changes in muscle length and speed of length change.

19. C: Range of motion refers to how far we can move our joints in different directions.

20. C: Ball-and-socket joints, like those found in hips and shoulders, allow for movement along multiple axes, providing a wide range of motion.

21. B: The origin refers to the end or attachment point of a muscle that remains relatively fixed during muscular contraction.

22. D: Voluntary muscle actions are those under conscious control, such as deciding to walk. Heart beating and diaphragm contracting are involuntary, and reflexes are automatic responses.

23. D: Range of motion exercises aim primarily at maintaining or increasing joint flexibility by ensuring full movement potential of a joint.

24. C: Fever is a systemic contraindication for massage because it indicates that the body is fighting an infection or illness. Massage could potentially spread the infection or exacerbate the condition.

25. A: Atherosclerosis involves the buildup of fats, cholesterol, and other substances in and on the artery walls which can lead to thickening and hardening, impacting blood flow.

26. C: Immediate postoperative periods are contraindications for massage as the tissues need time to heal and massage can disrupt this process.

27. B: While massage can be beneficial during the rehabilitation after a bone has properly healed from a recent fracture, it requires physician's approval to ensure that massage does not interfere with the healing process.

28. B: Lymphedema is caused by a blockage in the lymphatic system, which prevents lymph fluid from draining well, and this leads to swelling in the affected tissues.

29. B: Oncology massage is a specialized approach tailored to meet the unique needs of individuals who have been diagnosed with cancer or have cancer histories. It takes into account factors like treatment history, side effects, and potential risks.

30. A: Clients with diabetes can have reduced sensation in their feet and lower legs, making it necessary to use caution to avoid injury.

31. D: Deep abdominal pressure during pregnancy is avoided to prevent inducing labor, causing discomfort like nausea or potentially disrupting fetal development.

32. C: Post-surgery clients should be cleared by their physician before receiving a massage to ensure there are no contraindications.

33. C: Anticoagulants have blood-thinning effects, which could increase the risk of bruising when massaging a client on this type of medication.

34. B: Directly massaging over varicose veins can aggravate the condition; therefore, it's safer to avoid these areas or use very light pressure around them.

35. B: Clients with osteoporosis should not receive deep tissue massages due to the fragility of their bones that could easily fracture under intense pressure.

36. A: Corticosteroids can cause skin thinning and increase susceptibility to injury; therefore, deep pressure techniques should be avoided.

37. D: Clients undergoing chemotherapy may be more prone to lymphedema and have increased fragility due to their treatment, thus requiring careful consideration or avoidance of massage.

38. A: Soft tissue manipulation often results in a parasympathetic response, which can slow the heart rate.

39. A: Touch is known to release endorphins, providing psychological comfort and a sense of safety.

40. C: Soft tissue manipulation can help improve range of motion especially in conditions like arthritis.

41. C: The parasympathetic nervous system kicks in during soft tissue manipulation, resulting in a relaxation response.

42. C: Soft tissue manipulation is beneficial for athletes by helping reduce recovery time due to its effects on muscle relaxation and circulation.

43. B: Soft tissue manipulation can help reduce stress by lowering sympathetic nervous activity leading to a calm state.

44. C: Increased blood flow to the area as a result of soft tissue manipulation provides nutrients that nourish skin cells and enhance skin health.

45. A: Soft tissue manipulation can lead to reduced levels of neurotransmitters associated with pain sensation, providing relief from soreness and tension in pregnant women.

46. B: Soft tissue manipulation helps reduce edema (swelling caused by fluid retention), and improves lymphatic drainage, thereby aiding in post-operative recovery

47. C: Soft tissue manipulation techniques like massage are known to reduce muscle tension by breaking up adhesions, decreasing muscle spasms, and improving blood flow to the affected areas.

48. B: Cold therapy, also known as cryotherapy, helps reduce the tissue's metabolic rate, which can decrease inflammation and edema. This is often used for acute injuries to limit secondary tissue damage.

49. C: Manual lymphatic drainage (MLD) uses light touch to move excess lymph and fluid out of the tissues and back into the lymphatic vessels. This helps reduce swelling and improves immune function.

50. B: Myofascial release targets the fascial system with sustained pressure into myofascial restrictions. This helps to eliminate pain and restore motion by reducing compressive forces on nerves as fascial tension is released.

51. C: Hot stone massage uses smooth, heated stones that are placed or used as an extension of the therapist's hands to apply heat to specific areas on the body. The warmth relaxes muscles, improves circulation, and calms the nervous system.

52. C: Heat applications promote vasodilation which increases blood flow and nutrient delivery to tissues, whereas cold applications cause vasoconstriction which reduces blood flow to help decrease inflammation and pain.

53. B: Contraindications are conditions where a particular treatment should not be applied because it might be harmful. In particular, applying heat might exacerbate inflammation in case of acute injuries while applying cold can stiffen areas with chronic pain or restricted mobility.

54. C: Reviewing the written data provided by the client is crucial as it contains medical history, current health status, and specific issues or goals for the session that informs the subsequent steps of treatment.

55. B: Evaluating range of motion and posture are parts of a physical assessment that helps identify areas of tension or imbalance that need to be addressed in the massage treatment plan.

56. B: Reduced pain and increased mobility suggest positive progress, indicating that adjustments to reflect this improvement could benefit the ongoing treatment plan.

57. B: Written data enables customization of the treatment according to client-specific needs, conditions, and goals, thus improving effectiveness and safety.

58. B: Identifying contraindications is essential to prevent harm and ensure that chosen techniques/modalities are safe and appropriate for each individual client's condition.

59. B: Goal setting aligns both client and therapist expectations and guides decision-making regarding which therapies and techniques will best achieve those targets.

61. B: Regular reassessment allows for monitoring progress and making necessary adjustments to maximize therapeutic benefits throughout treatment.

61. C: While medical history, stress levels, and medications are relevant to assessing health status and risks, daily caloric intake is typically outside the scope required by massage therapists.

62. B: Kyphosis is characterized by an excessive outward curve of the spine, causing a hunching of the back. The visual indicators include rounded shoulders and a forward head position.

63. B: A dense and taut muscle upon palpation is often indicative of a muscle spasm, which is a sudden, involuntary contraction of the muscle fibers.

64. B: Frozen shoulder, or adhesive capsulitis, involves stiffness and limited movement in the shoulder joint, including limitations in abduction.

65. A: It's important for massage therapists to refer clients to other professionals when an issue presented by the client does not fall within their scope of practice or requires medical intervention that they are not qualified to give.

66. A: Reassessment helps to monitor progress and allows for adjustments to be made in the treatment plan according to any changes in the client's condition.

67. A: Inflammation typically involves an increase in local temperature due to increased blood flow as part of the body's immune response.

68. C: Current weather conditions are generally not relevant when conducting a clinical assessment which should focus on individual physiological and anatomical considerations.

69. A: Assessing range of motion can help identify joints or muscles with limitations or discomfort, indicating areas that may benefit from specific massage techniques.

70. C: Ethical behavior is fundamental in any practice, especially in massage therapy. It ensures that decisions and actions are made in the best interest of the client's health and safety, respecting their rights and maintaining a professional standard.

71. B: Boundaries are crucial for delineating the professional from the personal, establishing limits that protect both the client and therapist, and ensuring an effective and appropriate therapeutic relationship.

72. A: The code of ethics in massage therapy demands equal treatment for all clients. Refusing service based on discriminatory practices violates ethical standards designed to promote respect, fairness, and equality.

73. C: The therapeutic relationship refers to a professional, respectful alliance between therapist and client that focuses solely on the client's needs and treatment outcomes, without crossing into personal territory.

74. A: Dual relationships occur when there are multiple roles between a therapist and a client, such as being relatives or friends, which can jeopardize objectivity in treatment and risk boundary violations.

75. A: Beneficence is an ethical principle that involves acting with charity and goodness towards others; in massage therapy, it means doing what's beneficial for the client's health.

76. D: Part of maintaining ethical standards includes recognizing when treatment might cause emotional distress, addressing it sensitively by pausing treatment, demonstrating empathy, offering support or suggesting referrals to appropriate professionals.

77. B: If there's potential for an unethical dual relationship which could impair judgment or professionalism, therapists should set clear boundaries immediately or refer out to maintain professional integrity.

78. D: If a client suggests sexual services, it's important for the massage therapist to maintain professional boundaries. The therapist should end the session immediately, document the incident, and follow procedures that may include reporting it to a supervisor or appropriate authority.

79. B: Client confidentiality may be breached when there is a legal requirement such as a court order or subpoena. Otherwise, therapists must maintain confidentiality at all times.

80. B: Prescribing medication is not within the scope of practice for massage therapists and falls under medical professionals' responsibilities.

81. B: To maintain professionalism and avoid any implications of preferential treatment or influencing therapeutic relationships, therapists should politely decline gifts from clients.

82. C: Effective communication involves active listening, understanding clients' concerns, clarifying their goals for treatment, and formulating an appropriate therapy plan.

83. B: Accidental exposure of patient information should be treated seriously and reported immediately as an incident according to privacy laws.

84. C: Beneficence is an ethical principle that entails acting in ways that promote the welfare of clients, encouraging therapeutic actions that will provide benefit.

85. C: Professional communication involves addressing scheduling errors by contacting impacted clients directly to discuss alternative arrangements that accommodate their needs."

86. D: Pre-cleaning with soap and water is necessary to remove any physical debris before proper sanitization can occur.

87. A: To maintain hygienic conditions, the headrest cover should be changed after each client to prevent cross-contamination.

88. C: While maintaining cleanliness is essential, it is not required to use a fresh bottle of massage oil for every session; however, cross-contamination must be prevented.

89. D: A massage therapist should wash their hands both before and after a massage session to ensure sanitation and prevent cross-contamination.

90. C: EPA-registered disinfectants usually need to remain wet on the surface for about 5 minutes for effective sanitization, but it's important to follow specific product instructions.

91. B: Using disposable linens and wearing gloves will minimize the risk of spreading any potential infection without denying service.

92. C: Hot water settings are typically recommended when laundering used linens from massages to ensure that any pathogens are effectively eliminated.

93. B: Ensuring all electrical equipment is properly grounded minimizes electrocution risks, which is considered best safety practice.

94. C: Regular exercise and healthy eating are vital components of self-care that help prevent burnout by maintaining physical health and energy levels.

95. A: Draping techniques are used to maintain privacy, provide warmth, and create comfort for the client during a massage session.

96. C: Clear, professional communication regarding treatment plans, goals, and consent helps build trust between therapist and client, ensuring effective therapeutic outcomes.

97. C: Regular review of a business plan helps track progress, allows adjustments to be made due to changing circumstances, and ensures ongoing alignment with long-term goals.

98. A: SOAP notes are a method of documentation employed by healthcare providers including massage therapists to write out notes in a patient's chart.

99. B: Scope of practice refers to the legal framework outlining what services practitioners are permitted to perform in their professional role.

100. C: Liability insurance protects massage therapists against claims related to accidents or negligence that could occur during practice.

SCORING GUIDELINES

For the "MBLEx Practice Exams", the scoring guidelines allocate a percentage weight to various categories that reflect the content of the examination. The categories and their weights are as follows:

- ➤ Anatomy And Physiology: 11%
- ➤ Kinesiology: 12%
- ➤ Pathology, Special Populations, Contraindications, And Areas of Caution: 14%
- ➤ Benefits And Physiological Effects of Techniques That Manipulate Soft Tissue: 15%
- ➤ Client Assessment, Reassessment, And Treatment Plan Formulation: 17%
- ➤ Ethics, Laws, And Boundaries in Massage Therapy: 16%
- ➤ Guidelines For Professional Practice: 15%

Each category covers specific topics related to massage therapy, such as the function and structure of systems in anatomy and physiology, muscle contraction in kinesiology, clinical reasoning in client assessment, ethical behavior in ethics laws and boundaries, and proper use of equipment in professional practice guidelines. These percentages are reflective of how important each category is relative to the total examination and can be used as a focus guide for studying.

CHAPTER 12
TEST-TAKING STRATEGIES

STRATEGIES FOR APPROACHING MULTIPLE-CHOICE QUESTIONS

One of the most common types of questions you will encounter on the exam are multiple-choice questions (MCQs). These questions not only test your knowledge but also your test-taking skills. A standard multiple-choice question comprises a stem, which is the question or statement that requires completion or an answer, and a set of possible answers which include one correct option and several distractors. The distractors are there to test your knowledge and ability to discriminate between seemingly similar options.

Strategy 1. Read Carefully: The first strategy begins before answering any questions—read them carefully. Ensure that you understand what is being asked. This means paying close attention to key terms, qualifiers (such as 'always' or 'never'), and any specifics in the stem. Misreading or skimming can often lead to choosing an incorrect answer even when you know the right one.

Strategy 2. Answer In Your Mind First: After reading the question, try to anticipate the answer before looking at the options provided. This will help you remain unbiased by the choices presented and could make it easier to pick out the correct answer from the list.

Strategy 3. Use Process of Elimination: When faced with multiple options, use process of elimination to narrow down your choices. Disregard any answers that you know are incorrect. By eliminating these distractors, it increases your chances of choosing the correct option from those that remain.

Strategy 4. Lookout for Absolute Answers: Be cautious of answer choices that contain absolutes such as "all," "none," "always," or "never." These options are rarely correct as they demonstrate a level of certainty that isn't common in real-world scenarios. They can serve as clues when applying process of elimination.

Strategy 5. Consider All Options: Make sure you consider all available answers before making your selection—even if one seems right at first glance. Sometimes questions are designed to have two almost-correct answers where one is simply more complete or appropriate than the other.

Strategy 6. Don't Rush, But Don't Dawdle: Time management is critical during exams like MBLEX. While it is important not to rush through questions and risk careless mistakes, it's equally important not to spend too much time on a single question. If you're stumped, make an educated guess or mark it (if possible) and move on; you can always come back if time permits.

Strategy 7. Answer Every Question: Since there's usually no penalty for guessing on standardized exams like MBLEX, it's in your best interest to answer every question—even if you have to guess. An unanswered question is a guaranteed miss, but a guessed answer has a chance of being correct.

Strategy 8. Practice Good Exam Hygiene: Ensure that on exam day, you're well-rested and nourished, with all necessary supplies prepared ahead of time—including ID, admission ticket, pencils, erasers, etc.—so that once seated for your exam, all focus can be placed on tackling the test without any distractions or additional stressors.

Strategy 9. Stay Positive and Confident: Lastly, maintain a positive attitude throughout the exam. Confidence goes a long way in alleviating anxiety and helps improve recall ability during testing. Trust in your preparation leading up to test day and believe in yourself.

Remember that while these strategies are helpful, they're most effective when paired with thorough knowledge and understanding of massage therapy principles and practices covered in MBLEX test material. Thus, regular study combined with smart test-taking approaches forms a winning formula for success on exam day. Keep practicing these strategies during mock tests and review sessions; by doing so, they'll become second nature when you finally sit down to take your actual MBLEX Exam.

TIME MANAGEMENT TIPS

Managing your time effectively is a vital skill that can make all the difference when it comes to preparing for exams like the MBLEX. It's not just about studying hard—it's about studying smart. Below are various strategies that will help you to manage your time efficiently so you can maximize your chances of passing the MBLEX exam.

1. **Prioritize Your Study Goals:** Set a clear priorities for your MBLEX exam prep. Identify the topics that require more attention and those you're already comfortable with. Allocate more time to the areas that are challenging, while still reviewing what you know to keep it fresh in your memory.

2. **Create a Study Schedule:** Develop a study timetable that breaks down your MBLEX exam preparation into manageable chunks. Plan your study sessions during times when you are most alert and minimize distractions. Consistency is key; try to adhere to your schedule as much as possible.

3. **Use Time Blocks:** Divide your study sessions into specific time blocks dedicated to different subjects or topics. Pomodoro Technique, which uses 25-minute bursts of intense focus followed by short breaks, can be particularly effective. Adjust the duration of these blocks to suit your concentration span.

4. **Set Realistic Goals:** For each study session, set achievable goals that can be accomplished in the given time frame. This will help keep you motivated and give you a sense of progress as you prepare for the exam.

5. **Optimize Your Environment:** Create a conducive environment for studying by ensuring it is quiet, well-lit, and free from distractions. Inform family and friends of your study times so they can support you by minimizing interruptions during those periods.

6. **Limit Multitasking:** When multitasking, our brains cannot perform optimally on either task and it prolongs the overall study time. Focus on one subject at a time for better retention and greater productivity.

7. **Utilize Technology Wisely:** Use apps and tools designed to enhance productivity, such as digital flashcards, timers for keeping track of study sessions, or calendar apps to plan out your weeks leading up to the exam.

8. **Take Effective Breaks:** Make sure to rest between periods of intense study to avoid fatigue and mental burnout. Short breaks allow the brain to rest, leading to improved focus during subsequent study sessions.

9. **Review Regularly:** Regular review sessions are crucial for retaining information over time. Integrate regular review periods into your schedule to consolidate learning and ensure easier recall when taking the MBLEX exam.

10. **Be Flexible & Adapt:** Although having a well-structured plan is vital, be prepared to adapt if circumstances change or if a particular strategy is not working for you. Flexibility can help maintain momentum without causing additional stress.

11. **Manage Stress Effectively:** Include stress-relief techniques like deep breathing exercises or meditation in your daily routine, which will increase mental clarity and enhance concentration during your studies.

12. **Practice Time-Bound Exercises:** Simulate exam conditions by practicing with time-restricted quizzes or past papers to familiarize yourself with pacing during the actual MBLEX exam.

Remember that mastering time management is not just about stringent schedules; it's also about flexibility, understanding oneself, and being proactive in adapting methods that work best for individuals' learning styles and lifestyles.

CHAPTER 13
STUDY RESOURCES

RECOMMENDED BOOKS AND STUDY GUIDES

Here, we will guide you through a carefully curated list of recommended books and study guides that have been instrumental for many students in passing the MBLEX. These resources will help reinforce your knowledge, provide practice questions, and offer strategies to tackle the exam confidently.

1. "MBLEX Test Prep - Comprehensive Study Guide and Workbook, 2021" by David Merlino

David Merlino's comprehensive study guide is an invaluable resource for anyone preparing for the MBLEX. Its updated content reflects recent changes in the exam structure and provides a thorough overview of all the areas tested on the exam, including anatomy, physiology, kinesiology, and pathology. The workbook format encourages active learning with exercises, diagrams, and quizzes to test your understanding as you go along. Moreover, it includes detailed explanations of answers to help you grasp difficult concepts.

2. "Massage Therapy: Principles and Practice" by Susan G. Salvo

This textbook is a staple in massage therapy education. While not specifically an exam prep book, it is rich with information that covers key subjects for the MBLEX. Salvo's book dives deep into topics such as therapeutic relationships, ethics, business practices, and the various modalities within massage therapy – all of which are pertinent to a well-rounded understanding necessary for acing the exam.

3. "Trail Guide to the Body" by Andrew Biel

Understanding anatomy is a fundamental part of massage therapy and a significant portion of the MBLEX. "Trail Guide to the Body" is renowned among massage therapy students for its clear illustrations and detailed guide to palpation of muscles, ligaments, and bones. Using this book can enhance your practical knowledge of body structures, which is not only critical for passing the MBLEX but also essential for your future practice.

4. "MBLEx Flashcard Study System" by MBLEx Exam Secrets Test Prep Team

Flashcards remain one of the most effective study tools because they promote active recall, which is essential for retaining information. The "MBLEx Flashcard Study System" covers all aspects of the examination and can be used during any spare moment throughout your day – making study sessions both flexible and productive.

5. "Online Practice Exam from FSMTB"

The Federation of State Massage Therapy Boards (FSMTB) offers an online practice exam that replicates the format of the actual MBLEX. Since it's crafted by the same organization that administers the MBLEX, this practice test gives candidates an accurate expectation of what to encounter on exam day and helps them become familiar with navigating computer-based questions under timed conditions.

6. "Mosby's Massage Therapy Review" by Sandy Fritz

Sandy Fritz has compiled this review book that serves as an excellent tool for quick study sessions or reviews before taking your test. It includes numerous choice questions that reflect those found on MBLEX across all categories covered in the examination – ensuring that you get ample practice dealing with specific areas where you might need more focus.

7. "Anatomy & Physiology: The Massage Connection" by Kalyani Premkumar

This book emphasizes understanding how physiology relates to massage treatments – a vital aspect examined in MBLEX. Its clear explanations make complex physiological processes accessible to learners at all levels while providing context as to why such knowledge applies directly to their future work as massage therapists.

Each recommended resource has its strengths in helping you master different aspects of what's covered on the MBLEX—from theoretical foundations to practical applications in massage therapy practice. By using these books and study guides in conjunction with each other, students can gain comprehensive knowledge through multiple perspectives and varied learning methods.

It's important not only just read through these resources but actively engage with them—taking notes, doing practice tests under timed conditions, highlighting key points for revision at a later time, participating in study groups or discussions online or offline with peers also preparing for their exams.

Remember that while self-study is important, sometimes attending a review course or seeking help from educators or fellow students might give you additional insights or clarification on topics that seem challenging.

By methodically working through these recommended books and study guides while also utilizing available tools such as flashcards and practice tests, aspiring massage therapists can establish a solid foundation of knowledge upon which they can build a successful career.

ONLINE RESOURCES AND PRACTICE TESTS

One of the most effective ways to ensure success is to harness the power of online resources and practice tests. These digital tools offer a rich environment for learning, practice, and self-evaluation, helping students to refine their knowledge and approach the exam with confidence.

Online resources come in many forms, from interactive modules and e-books to video lectures and virtual flashcards. They allow for a tailored approach to studying, enabling students to focus on areas where they need improvement. Websites such as the National Certification Board for Therapeutic Massage & Bodywork (NCBTMB) provide a wealth of information, including guidelines on exam content and recommended reading materials.

One significant advantage of online resources is their convenience; they can be accessed anywhere at any time. This means studying can be seamlessly integrated into daily life, whether during a lunch break or on public transport. Such flexibility ensures that valuable study time is maximized, and learning becomes a continuous process.

Moreover, online resources often include forums and discussion groups where candidates can connect with each other. These communities provide moral support and a platform where students can ask questions, share insights, and exchange study tips. Engaging with peers who are also preparing for the MBLEX can offer fresh perspectives and new strategies for mastering complex topics.

When it comes to practice tests, online platforms provide an array of benefits over traditional paper exams. They simulate the actual testing environment, giving candidates a sense of the timing and format of the real MBLEX. By regularly taking timed practice tests online, students can build test-taking stamina and learn how to manage exam pressure effectively.

Online practice tests also offer immediate feedback on performance. This instant grading allows learners to identify their strengths and weaknesses in real-time, enabling them to adjust their study plans accordingly. Furthermore, because online tests are typically generated from a large bank of questions, students are less likely to encounter repeat questions. This variety ensures a broad coverage of topics and keeps the practice experience fresh and challenging.

Adaptive learning technology is another feature that sets online practice tests apart. Some platforms use algorithms to adjust the difficulty level of questions based on an individual's performance. As a result, students receive a personalized learning experience that targets their unique needs.

Of particular note are full-length online MBLEX simulations that mimic the structure and time constraints of the actual exam. Engaging with these simulations helps students become familiar with the pacing required to complete each section within the allotted time frame without sacrificing accuracy or composure. This familiarity avoids any surprises on test day and allows candidates to address any time management issues beforehand.

Finally, analytics provided by these platforms play a crucial role in studying effectiveness. After completing practice tests or learning modules, students can access detailed reports that outline various metrics such as scores over time, question categories where they excel or underperform, and suggested areas for further study. These analytics help contextualize performance in a way that guides more focused review sessions.

By combining convenience with interactivity, instant feedback with personalized learning paths, and community support with sophisticated analytics – these technologies not only enhance learning outcomes but also turn the daunting task of preparing for such an important examination into an engaging and manageable endeavor.

CHAPTER 14
POST-EXAM STEPS

RECEIVING YOUR MBLEX SCORES

After you have navigated the nerve-racking waters of examination day and emerged on the other side, a period of anticipation follows. Typically, one of the most pressing questions on candidates' minds is: "How long must I wait to know my results?" The Federation of State Massage Therapy Boards (FSMTB), which administers the exam, strives to deliver scores expediently.

In most cases, your unofficial MBLEX scores are available immediately after completing the test. However, these provisional scores are not the basis for your licensing decision. You will receive an official results report, which is usually sent electronically to your state board within 24 hours after completing your examination.

Understanding how your MBLEX scores are reported is essential. The MBLEX uses a scaled scoring system—this means that your raw score (the number of questions you answered correctly) is converted into a scaled score that falls between 300 and 900 points. The magic number to watch for is 630—the minimum scaled score required to pass. This scaling system accounts for minor variations in exam difficulty and ensures fairness across different administrations of the test.

Upon receiving your scores, it's natural for a myriad of emotions to cascade through you. If your official report signifies success, breathe a sigh of relief and allow yourself a moment of prideful reflection on the hard work that brought you here. However, if the news is less positive and you didn't achieve the passing score needed, be kind to yourself. It's important to recognize that a setback on the MBLEX is not a reflection of your potential as a future massage therapist but merely an indication that there are areas in need of further review and deeper understanding.

A second attempt awaits when you're ready; it's merely another step in your professional journey. The FSMTB permits candidates to retake the exam after 30 days have passed since their last attempt. Use this time wisely—hone in on weak areas indicated by your score report, consolidate your knowledge foundations, and perhaps seek out additional resources or support.

Once you've passed the MBLEX and received confirmation from both FSMTB and your state board confirming licensure eligibility, it's time to turn towards launching your career. Begin researching employment opportunities or lay groundwork for starting a private practice if that's where your aspirations lead. Fulfill any remaining state requirements, such as background checks or additional documentation submissions. Then proceed with applying for licensure through your state board—an act that officially marks the beginning of your professional career as a licensed massage therapist.

For international graduates or candidates trained outside the U.S., receiving results can involve extra layers. Your path may include transcript evaluation services or additional verification steps by regulatory boards specific to where you were trained compared to where you intend to practice. Consult with both FSMTB guidelines and local state board requirements well in advance to ensure all necessary actions are completed seamlessly after passing the exam.

Receiving your MBLEX scores marks not an end but an exhilarating commencement—the dawn of professional empowerment and transformative possibilities within healthcare's healing realm.

Remember that test results arrive cloaked in objectivity; they do not measure passion nor predict future success. The data simply assesses current knowledge against standardized criteria. Embrace every outcome as an instructive moment propelling personal growth—the same growth that defines every skilled practitioner's evolution within this noble field.

NEXT STEPS AFTER PASSING THE EXAM

Congratulations! You've surmounted the mountain that is the Massage and Bodywork Licensing Examination (MBLEX). As you hold your passing results in hand, it's natural to feel a refreshing mix of relief and exhilaration. Your dedication to studying the intricacies of anatomy, physiology, kinesiology, pathology, and client assessment has paid off. But what do you do after the elation subsides? This new chapter of your career beckons you to take practical steps forward.

Take a moment to savor your success. Passing the MBLEX is a milestone in your journey as a professional massage therapist. Let family and friends celebrate your achievement; their support has been invaluable throughout your studies.

After the celebrations wane, it's time to focus on the administrative side of things. Securely file away your exam results for future reference. This document serves as proof of your academic accomplishments and may be required for state licensure or potential employment.

Speaking of licensure, step two is to apply for it. Each state has its specific requirements post-MBLEX for gaining a license to practice. Ensure you are familiar with these details by visiting your state's massage therapy board website or contacting them directly via phone or email. The typical documents required include your examination score report, proof of education—transcripts or diplomas from your massage therapy program—and possibly background checks or fingerprinting.

Part of being licensed may also entail obtaining liability insurance. This not only protects you in case of any legal action from clients but also is oftentimes mandated by states or employers before you start practicing.

Now that the formalities are underway, turn your attention to career planning. If you haven't done so already during your training period, start researching potential employment opportunities. Spas, wellness centers, chiropractic offices, fitness clubs, and private practices are common places where massage therapists find work. You may also want to explore unconventional paths such as working on cruise ships or in luxury resorts if travel interests you.

Prepare an up-to-date resume highlighting your educational background, skills learned during internships or practical components of your study program, relevant work experience—even non-massage-related positions can showcase valuable soft skills—and obviously, include successful completion of the MBLEX.

Furthermore, establish a professional online presence by creating profiles on job search platforms and on professional networks like LinkedIn. Emphasize not only your technical massage skills but also any secondary offerings like aromatherapy or reflexology that make you stand out.

Networking shouldn't be neglected either. Attend industry conferences or local meetups to connect with established therapists and businesses in need of fresh talent. Joining professional associations can also provide leads on jobs and continuing education opportunities; they can keep you up-to-date with industry trends essential for long-term success in this field.

The realm of continuous education awaits! Like any healthcare-related profession, staying current with latest practices will be critical in delivering quality care and maintaining licensure via credits for renewal. Explore workshops, additional certifications or advanced courses that align with areas where you wish to specialize or grow professionally.

Lastly but importantly – hone your business acumen if self-employment intrigues you. Drafting a business plan, understanding marketing techniques to attract clients, managing finances responsibly – these are entrepreneurial skills vital for those planning to open their own practice.

This is just a sketch; remember that everyone's post-exam path will look different based on personal goals and circumstances. But regardless of direction chosen after passing the MBLEX exam - whether immediately entering the workforce or taking additional time for growth - one thing is sure: You've earned a significant victory which lays a strong foundation for an impactful career as a licensed massage therapist. Now it's time to use that hard-earned knowledge in healing bodies and spirits—one session at a time.

CONCLUSION

Congratulations on completing your journey through this comprehensive MBLEx Exam Prep book. By reaching here, you've shown tremendous dedication and resilience in your pursuit of excellence within the field of massage therapy. The effort you've invested in mastering the content of this guide reflects not only your commitment to personal development but also your unwavering dedication to providing top-tier care to your future clients.

As you turn this final page, remember that this is not the end of your learning path but rather a significant milestone. The field of massage therapy is dynamic and ever-evolving, and it is fueled by passionate practitioners like you who continually seek to enhance their expertise and refine their craft.

The knowledge you've acquired here is a strong foundation upon which you will build your professional practice. Every chapter that detailed anatomy, physiology, pathology, bodywork techniques, ethics, and laws has equipped you with the tools necessary to excel not only in the MBLEx exam but also in your day-to-day responsibilities as a massage therapist.

Taking the MBLEx was an essential step in legitimizing your expertise and opening doors to opportunities that will allow you to make meaningful impacts on health and wellness. As you step into this next phase, embracing lifelong learning will be key to sustaining success. Stay curious; continue to pursue advanced certifications, workshops, and seminars that can broaden your skills and deepen your understanding of bodywork. Networking with other professionals can also provide invaluable insights and support as you navigate through the various aspects of your career. Join professional massage therapy associations, attend conferences, and connect with mentors who can guide you toward fulfilling opportunities for growth.

Remember that self-care is just as important as client care. Practicing what you preach by maintaining your own well-being enables you to be an exemplary model of health for your clients. A balanced lifestyle will ensure that you are always at your best both physically and mentally to provide exceptional service. Finally, let gratitude be at the core of everything you do. Thank those who have supported you thus far—your teachers, peers, family—and keep a grateful heart for the privilege to impact lives positively through your work. Your hands have the power to heal, comfort, and restore; wield them with confidence and compassion.

Made in the USA
Monee, IL
26 November 2024

71321058R00057